Yarn Harlot

Yarn Harlot

the secret life of a knitter

stephanie pearl-mcphee

**Andrews McMeel
Publishing**

Kansas City

05 06 07 08 09 FFG 10 9 8 7 6 5 4 3 2 1

ISBN-13: 978-0-7407-5037-3
ISBN-10: 0-7407-5037-2

Library of Congress Control Number: 2005048052

Book design by Holly Camerlinck

www.andrewsmcmeel.com

Attention: Schools and Businesses

Andrews McMeel books are available at quantity discounts with bulk purchase for
educational, business, or sales promotional use. For information, please write to:
Special Sales Department, Andrews McMeel Publishing, 4520 Main Street, Kansas
City, Missouri 64111.

This one is for my grampa, James Alexander McPhee.
He was the first writer I knew.

Introduction   xi

one

The Red Wool of Courage:
Or, Projects I Have Known and Loved   **1**

    The Green Afghan   2

    The Wedding Sweater Saga   11

    The Cardigan Letter   27

    The Thing About Socks   31

    The Sheep Shawl   35

    The Entrelac Socks   41

two

Twenty Thousand Skeins Under the Bed:
Or, Stash and Why You Want It   **45**

    The Beast   46

    Cracking the Whip   54

Nothing in My Stash	60
Mine, Mine, All Mine	64
If You Have a Lot of Yarn . . .	67
The System	72
Moth	76

three

Dangerous Liaisons: Or, Yarn Can Be Addictive	**87**
Archaeology	88
Spring Is Sprung	94
How to Succeed at Knitting (Without Really Trying)	99
Yarn Requirements	103
"IT"	106
Sour Grapes	115
Socks for Sinead	120

four

War and Pieces: Or, You Can't Win Them All	**133**
What Her Hands Won't Do	134
Freakin' Birds	140
Operation: Cast On	145
I Can Do That	148
One Little Sock	153
What Passes for Perfect	157
Veni Vidi Steeki	162
Good Morning, Class	173

five

My Family, and Other Works in Progress   **177**

The Rules   178

What She Gave Me   184

Ten Ways to Anger a Knitter   190

This Makes More Sense   192

Three Blankets   196

Resister   202

Parents and Knitters   204

Is This a Test?   206

DPN   212

Acknowledgments   **221**

$\mathcal{I}$ am a person who works well under pressure. In fact, I work so well under pressure that at times, I will procrastinate in order to create this pressure. Naturally, as with all human failings, this system of procrastination occasionally backfires and creates more pressure than I had really intended. Such was the case a week before the manuscript for this book was due. I had accidentally created a little bit more pressure than was really wise, and as a result had been reduced to writing day and night, only stopping to complain to my family (who were pleased as punch that it had come down to this again) about having to write a book day and night.

At about the time that I had started to order pizza for several meals in a row and the family began to ask me ever so delicately if I ever intended to do a load of laundry again, I took my laptop (and a glass of decent merlot—though perhaps we should forget that) up to my bedroom. After a hot bath, I ensconced myself, delirious and exhausted, in my bed to write the introduction to this book.

I began to type then—it was something completely trite, I'm sure, though I've now forgotten. The next thing I remember was my lovely husband gently waking me up by pulling my sleeping face off the laptop. The next morning, when I returned to the screen, I discovered that somehow, as I slept with my face on the keyboard, my nose had typed seventeen pages of the letter *Y*.

Initially I didn't see the poetry in that. Perhaps if I had somehow managed to fill seventeen pages with *J*, I would still be stuck. But now, I see the gift my slumbering nose presented. There is Meaning here. There is Significance.

"Why" indeed? Why was I killing myself over a book about the joy of knitting? Why have I had, over the course of decades, a love affair with knitting that consumes me so completely? Why would any sane person give up so much closet space and money to a craft that seems simple and silly?

The answer: Because knitting is more than it seems. Knitting is a complex and joyful act of creation in my everyday life.

It really does seem so simple. Knitting is only two stitches, knit and purl, yet with those two ordinary acts we knitters can take a ball of yarn and a couple of pointy sticks and create something useful and beautiful. An average sweater takes God-only-knows-how-many stitches to make, each one of them a simple act. Wrapping yarn around needles over and over and over again disconnects me from my cares. Knitting makes something from nothing, and it's usually such an *interesting* something.

Even when it isn't going well, knitting can be deeply spiritual. Knitting sets goals that you can meet. Sometimes when I work on something complicated or difficult—ripping out my work and starting over, poring over tomes of knitting expertise, screeching "I don't get it!" while practically weeping with frustration—my husband looks at me and says, "I don't know why you think you like knitting." I just stare at him. I don't *like* knitting. I *love* knitting. I don't know what could have possibly led him to think that I'm not enjoying myself. The cursing? The crying? The fourteen sheets of shredded graph paper? Knitting is like a marriage (I tell him) and you don't just trash the whole thing because there are bad moments.

I love knitting because it's something that can be accomplished no matter how poorly it's going at any given moment. It's a triumph of dexterity over string. I can't make my kids turn out the way I want; I have no control over my editor; world peace remains elusive despite my very best efforts; but all of that be damned—I can put a heel in a sock and it will go exactly the way I want it to go. Eventually, at least.

Knitting is magic. Knitting is an act of creation and a simple transformation each and every time. Each knitted gift holds hours of my life. I know it looks just like a hat, but really, it's four hours at the hospital, six hours on the bus, two hours alone at four in the morning when I couldn't sleep because I tend to worry. It is all those hours when I chose to spend time warming another person. It's giving them my time—time that I could have spent on anything, or anyone, else. Knitting is love, looped and warm.

So—why this book? Because there are fifty million knitters in North America. I can't be the only one who feels this way.

Raise your needles (straight or circular) if you're with me.

one

The Red Wool of Courage:
Or, Projects I Have Known and Loved

The Green Afghan

$\mathscr{I}$ am, by most accounts, a normal woman. It's possible that I have a little more yarn than is really the national average, but lots of people have an obsession. I like deadlines, I work well under pressure, and procrastination runs in my family the way that tone deafness runs in others. I have an aunt or two a little on the odd side and an uncle who played the ukulele, but as far as I know, there is no family history of insanity. We are, however, really big dreamers, and I wonder if that is what started this whole thing.

You've heard of the Red Scourge? the Black Death? the Yellow Plague? Meet my nemesis, the Green Afghan.

My brother Ian proposed to a woman I adored and set a date for the first wedding in our family for years. I was completely thrilled. The woman in question, Alison, is not only kind, gentle, and clever, but had demonstrated one of the finest qualities in a potential sister-in-law: an appreciation for handknits. In fact (not that I was snooping around or anything, that would be wrong), I had noticed that there were handknit pillows on her couch. This, together with my brother's love of all things woolly and warm and my natural knitterly inclination to demonstrate my love with yarn, made my path clear. I would knit them a wedding present.

I started thinking about the possibilities. The wedding was five months away and I felt pretty darned sure that I could finish just about anything in five months. I mulled it over: 150 days, 3,600 hours. I started thinking big. I thought about "His and Hers" sweaters. I thought about knitting lace edges for pillow cases. I thought about a hundred things. I considered matching socks, really beautiful ones, but rejected that idea when I thought about it further. Socks wear out. What sort of omen would it be if they walked huge honkin' holes in their wedding socks by their third anniversary? I imagined them looking at the holes, then looking at each other, and wondering if it was a sign. Whatever I knit, it had to be enduring. Something they would use, something that would be cozy for both of them, something that would last a long time. Something that would last long enough that they'd still treasure it on their fiftieth anniversary (or at least something they'd both fight for in divorce court).

I started to think about an afghan. You can't outgrow a blanket; it can't be the wrong size, and it would last a whole marriage if I used good wool and gave them a stern lecture on how to wash it. They could still be using it a long time from now if I picked a classic color.

Everybody's got a lime, gold, and orange granny-square afghan that Aunt Shirley crocheted for you in 1973. It's the afghan that you never throw over yourself when you have a hangover, since it turns the headache into a pounding so violent that you can actually feel your hair grow. Instead you've got it jammed in the hall closet on the top shelf. You take it out twice a year: Once when you've got a friend staying on the couch and you are desperate for an extra blanket, and once when your aunt Shirley's daughter Enid comes over and you artfully drape it over the couch so she can't catch you out.

I didn't want to be Aunt Shirley. I made a note to myself that I would try to pick something really chastely classic. I sat down with my pattern books and started thinking it over. What to do? I wanted something interesting enough that I could stand to knit it, but not so interesting that it would get tedious. A wedding afghan must absolutely be big enough to cover the both of them so I'd make the thing about eight by five feet. (Please note that I was, in fact, aware that most afghans are about three and one half feet by five feet. I have absolutely no explanation for why I chose to make this behemoth so big, except that I really love my brother and sometimes the expression of love in wool needs to be little oversized. Also, I may be insane.) That meant that whatever pattern I chose, I'd have to knit forty square feet of it. Forty square feet of garter stitch is a knitter's lobotomy. Brain damage would inevitably ensue. I have jammed projects into permanent imprisonment in the hall closet for less. I had to be careful too. Ian and Alison wouldn't like something frilly or fussy. They are not "doily" types, and if you can find a speck of lace in their house I'll give you a dollar. I needed plain, but not too plain, and interesting, but not too interesting.

I settled on a pattern that started with small squares. Four squares came together to form a larger geometric shape; these big squares were joined with vine-patterned strips in between, then a leaf border went around the whole thing. The modular aspect meant that the whole thing would stay portable until I started doing the strips and the border. I was looking forward to it. It was going to be stunning and totally doable in five months.

At the yarn store I started realizing the enormity of the project. I was going to need almost thirty balls of wool. That's a lot of yarn. That's so much yarn that when I told the yarn store lady what I needed, she let out a low whistle and gave me a look that told me that she thought that maybe when I'm not knitting over-sized afghans I amused myself by trying to pick up marbles with chopsticks. It's so much that she had to go into the basement to look for two cases of the yarn in question. As she stacked the yarn on the counter she seemed a little incredulous. This should have been my first warning: When a person who sells yarn for a living thinks that maybe you're buying a lot of yarn—well, it's a sign. A different sort of knitter would have taken that as a hint. Me? I thought she was a knitter without aspirations.

The price tag for the enormous bag of yarn was dizzying, but I shrugged it off. I wrestled my new yarn out of the shop (ignoring the stares of the new knitter over by the mohair who was buying a single ball of something blue and clearly thought I might be dangerous). Forcing the yarn through the door of the bus, trying to avoid whacking people with it, I decided that it was worth it. My brother was getting married. It's beautiful yarn and I was knitting an heirloom that would last forever, and, furthermore (my furthermores are always a sign of really bad thinking), I do like a challenge.

At home I dumped the big pack of yarn onto the couch and looked at it. For the first time I faltered a little. This project was going to require miles and miles of knitting. I started trying to figure out where I was going to keep the yarn while I worked on it. My living room is pretty tiny, and this was taking up a sizable chunk of real estate. *At least I like the color,* I thought, as I considered replacing the throw pillow stuffing with balls of yarn. I'd chosen a deep green, green enough to count as a color, but muted, like the greens in the shadows of a pine forest. It was manly enough that my brother wouldn't get nervous, bright enough that my new sister-in-law would think it was pretty, and plain enough that there will have to be a room in their new house that it would match. It was classic.

I found my 4-millimeter needles and cast on the first square, ignoring that part of my brain that noted that bigger needles would make the work go faster. This was not a project for short-cuts. I worked the pattern, humming to myself. The yarn was good, the pattern intriguing . . . I bet I'd finish it next week. I wouldn't be able to drag myself from it. Sure enough, at the end of the day I had two squares done. *Two down,* I thought proudly. I felt a pang when I finished the sentence. One hundred and fifty-eight to go.

The next day dawned bright, and so did my enthusiasm. All day I knit, wrote, and did laundry. At the end of the day, with really very little effort, I had three more squares. The pang eased. If I kept this up, this was going to be a walk in the park. The wedding was in about 150 days, and I had about 150 squares to knit, and I was managing at least two a day. No problem. That meant that all the squares would be knit in half the time, and then I'd have the rest of the time for the strips between the squares and the border. I stopped just short of giggling. (Those with experience in these matters would recognize my overconfidence at this point as "foreshadowing." You know, like the moment in a horror movie when the attractive young man turns to his girlfriend and mocks her for worrying about the ax murderer on the loose. You just know he's got a date with destiny.)

The next day, well, the next day I didn't knit any squares at all. In fact, since I had so much time, I didn't knit any for a week. I did, however, make a really cool pair of socks, and then a hat, and then I started a new sweater . . . Suddenly a month had gone by. My mother dropped by and I decided to tell her about the afghan. Maybe if someone else knew about it I'd feel pressured. When I explained my plan to turn the mountain of green yarn into squares just like the five on the table, she laughed. I ignored her. She doesn't knit, and she doesn't know about these things. She thinks that *all* knitting was "a lot of knitting." This was still a doable project. I just needed motivation.

After she left (still chuckling), I went and got the big bag of greenness and settled back in again. It turned out that a change was as good as a rest. It was at least, oh, four or five more squares before it started to wear a little thin on me again. (By "wear a little thin," I mean that I felt the urge to have a drink or five to take the edge off the way my teeth itched when I worked on it.) I began to dream in green.

When I had knit thirty-four squares I realized that I'd managed to commit the pattern to memory. This was a small victory, but one that at least reassured me that no matter how it felt, the impression that the afghan was melting holes in my brain must be an illusion.

By the sixtieth square I'd started to play little games with myself. I could knit a round of my sock when I finished a square. I could work on the sweater for an hour when I had four squares done. I raced myself to get the best possible time on a square. The afghan lurked in its enormous, ominous way all the time, especially when I tried to ignore it. I beat down the first waves of resentment. After all, it was not as if I'd been forced to knit it at gunpoint. It was my decision to knit the biggest freaking unmercifully huge afghan in the universe. I was the one who thought it would be fun. I was the one who was going to stick with it. I was no quitter.

When I woke up one morning and discovered that the thought of knitting another green square made me feel inexplicably sad, I put it back into the closet. I had three months to go, and there was no reason for this to get ugly. I apologized to the children for the swearing they may have heard as I looked for a space big enough to put the afghan in. I apologized under my breath to Ian and Alison. I had to try harder to put good karma into this. I wanted something enduring, comfortable, and reassuring. Now I was knitting all these "I can't stand you; when will this nightmare ever end?" vibes into it. That couldn't be the sort of sentiment you'd want to wish on a marriage. I'd work on the sweater until the involuntary shudder that I felt each time I thought of the afghan went away.

A month passed, and the afghan and I began to forgive each

other. It stopped leaping from the closet each time I tried to get a towel out, and I stopped saying curse words while I shoved it back in with my foot, hoping that moths would get it. My mother inquired about it occasionally, so I spent some of my knitting time looking in the mirror and perfecting a blank, unknowing stare that said "What afghan?"

When I could no longer justify pretending that the green amorphous blob in the linen closet was a pool cover, I started working on it again. I was careful not to overdo it, since I felt that my dislike of the thing was like frostbite: Once you've had a dose you are very vulnerable to it. I knew that if I caught the green flu again, there might be no way back. I wouldn't dream of not finishing, so I worked out rewards. I tried pairing the afghan with things that I enjoyed, but mixing it with red wine was trouble (friends don't let friends knit drunk . . . that square was, well, not very square). I tried bribing myself with chocolate, but quickly realized that if you promise yourself a bite of chocolate after every row of a five-by-eight-foot afghan—well, let's just say that it might not be such an oversized blanket after all.

As the deadline neared I began to worry. (By "worry" I mean I obsessed about it every waking moment of my life.) I was almost done with the squares, but I hadn't started the strips that joined the squares. We weren't even discussing who I thought was going to sew this thing together. I was starting to feel like maybe when I knit on it I was giving myself an aneurysm. It was horrible. Licking a yak would be more fun. The evening that I realized that there wasn't a circular needle in the world big enough to hold all of the border stitches just about finished me.

I didn't quit, although I did start to hallucinate a little. As I glared at the ocean of green in my lap, I thought about orange. Orange merino, orange like tangerines; yellow like canaries sitting on pomegranates outlined against the bluest sky and sea. I tried to think of anything not green. A bowl of red grapes in a cerulean bowl, set on a terra-cotta table. Persimmons laid on a quilt of gold and white. Strawberries, blueberries, lemons. Pink roses.

I kept knitting. I started sewing. I bought four circular needles for the innumerable border stitches. I knit green until walking by grass annoyed me and salad filled me with hostility, and then I knit more green.

Weeks later I watched Ian and Alison open their wedding present. I was filled with pride and joy on this special day. I knew that I'd done the right thing. They opened their gift and beamed at me across the room.

Everybody needs a punchbowl.

The Wedding Sweater Saga

March 18
Starting the Sweaters.

This week has been some of the most satisfying knitting of my life. In November my good friend Ken took up knitting. In a massive show of love, he knit me a pair of socks and now proudly wears the title "knitter."

This past week some friends announced that they were taking the plunge and getting married in June. Ken decided that we should knit matching wedding sweaters for them. We bought the yarn, and happily cast on. Even though the pattern was complex, it made sense; it had a logical progression that was easy to follow. One repeat of sixteen rows and neither of us needed to look at the chart anymore.

I cannot express the delight I'm taking in sitting beside my dear friend, knitting away on a cool pattern with yummy yarn, and discussing the whole thing with him and *actually having him care*! He's always had the grace to pretend that he cared about knitting, but it's different when you know he's just not being polite. I've been raving about it all week. This is going to be so much fun!

Now, if we could just stop competing for who's farther along . . .

April 7
An Open Letter to a Famous Designer, AbFabFibers, Inc.

Dear Famous Designer,

Straight off the bat, let me tell you how very much I admire your work. My friend and I are knitting a matched set of his and her sweaters for our friends who are getting married in June. The pattern is inspired and the charts are very clear and easy to work from. You are truly a knitting goddess.

This genuine admiration of your work makes it all the more shocking that I have now been plunged into anxious despair.

I painstakingly read your instructions and carefully followed your chart and made my way through the back of the sweater. It ended, as you instructed, by decreasing purlwise across a right-side row. This finish looked a little odd, but I decided that the purl stitches across the shoulder look charming, especially given the inspired sleeve shaping with the strap that will knit into the shoulder seam—yes, you are clever, dear designer. Truly, an innovative design feature. You are my guide and I will follow your genius wherever it may lead.

That said, I embarked on the front, knitting ahead of my less experienced friend, taking careful notes so that our work will match. I gleefully approached the neck shaping, dutifully stopping fourteen rows short of where I did for the back, just as you said. Except . . . now, Designer—not that I would doubt you for a moment, surely it is just that your own aptitude for this exceeds my own—if I follow your instructions for shaping the neck, I end up running that charming row of purl decreases across the wrong side, not across the right side as in the back. I also had to fuss with the number of rows to make it end on the wrong side, but let's just deal with the bigger issues here.

It could very well be that you do not like the front and back to match. This must surely be the case, as you specifically instruct me to work the purls across the right side on the back, and the wrong side on the front. It seems to me that this will make knitting in the shoulder strap odd-looking indeed, but this may all be part of the creative process, and part of the wonder of knitting a sweater of note.

I have (very briefly) considered the possibility of a mistake in the pattern, but I can't be sure, as the artistic photos of the sweater being worn by very attractive people show off the feel of the sweater to its best advantage, but they don't let me compare front and back to figure out what's up here.

The other alternative is that all will be revealed in the fullness of time and perhaps if I just continue to follow with the blindness of a zealot, when I get to the shoulder strap it will all make perfect sense and I will once again bow and scrape to the wonder that is you. That's a long way off though, and I'd like a little more reassurance.

So, dear designer, if you are out there, I'd just like your home phone number so that maybe I could call you when these little things come up.

Your faithful servant,
Stephanie

April 19
Disaster.

When we decided on the Wedding Sweaters pattern, we chose
our yarns: a lovely light gray for me to knit for the bride and a
darker gray yarn for Ken to use for the groom. There was careful calculation, much discussion, and eventually consensus at
the time of purchase. Ken, the yarn shop owner, and I all felt that
there was enough of the dark gray to pull it off. There really
should have been, as we even used a calculator to figure the
yardage. We bought all the yarn shop had and boldly embarked
on the Wedding Sweater Scheme.

As a new knitter, Ken has been terribly excited and has had
to work very hard to stay on track for the deadline. He's had to
knit in public, knitting away on the streetcar on the way to work.
Another man commented "That's very brave," the first sign that
Ken's sense of masculinity must be strong to endure this trial.
The general consensus among our intimates is that, for a man,
knitting in public is probably the closest you can get to wearing
a KICK ME sign. Despite the obvious peril and a lot of ripping his
work back, he's still gung ho. Each row of the front and back
took him fifteen minutes, and still both pieces are finished.

On Saturday, he began the sleeves, and dipped into his stash
box (Isn't that cute, his stash fits into a box!) for a new ball.
Shock, horror, and bewilderment! He's only got three balls of the
yarn left, with two sleeves and the neck to go. Clearly, he is not
going to make it.

Now that the shock has worn off, we're trying to deal with

the disaster. Only other knitters can grasp the kind of strain the poor man is under. It's his first sweater, he's on a deadline, he's risked his life knitting in public, and now his strength of character won't help him. He's encountered one of the universal knitting nightmares. He's run out of yarn and *we can't find more.*

I don't know about you, but I don't think enough men knit. I think that I am blessed in having a friend who is well on his way to understanding the obsession, and will even say things like, "Wanna go to the yarn shop?" with a gleam in his eye and eagerness oozing from him. How many knitters have this? This one bad experience could put him off knitting forever.

Do it for him, or do it for me—but, please, check your stashes.

We need AbFabFibers "Simply Smashing"; color 53, lot 218. It's a DK weight, in a charcoal gray. We are willing to pay, beg, grovel, trade my firstborn, sing your praises from the highest mountain, walk your dog—whatever you want—just send me the yarn.

May 19
The Yarn Hunt.

First and foremost an important announcement: KEN FINISHED HIS WEDDING SWEATER LAST NIGHT!

He informs me that we can't call it a finished object until I've done the making up, but I'm so proud of him that I could just bust. Other than the total meltdown over the yarn shortage (read on for the full story), which is completely understandable, Ken didn't whine, complain, or beg for sympathy through this entire thing. He's a new knitter and certainly not fast. I think he deserves a medal. The sweater looks great. It's worth noting that he finished before me (I think that's especially important to him).

I shudder to think of the time that I spent calling and e-mailing to find this yarn. The basic upshot is that there was no yarn in this dye lot left on the planet. I'm sure of this. I don't know where it all is, or who was holding out on us, but there was not a ball to be had. Eventually, I discovered that the original yarn shop had two balls of the correct color but the wrong dye lot, and a not-so-local yarn shop had three. We planned a reconnaissance mission. Ken and I borrowed a car, put my three kids in it, and set off bravely. He was still unsure about my complex plan to combine dye lots, but I assured him (with a remarkable degree of feigned confidence) that all would be well.

The original yarn shop had promised us one ball of the correct lot and one ball of another lot. In a stunning and traumatic development, the shop had nothing left of the original. Instead, we were offered a ball of a dye lot so far from the original that Ken was left crouching by the car, head between his knees, gasping for air. I comforted Ken (again with that remarkable air of false confidence) and we accepted the other stray ball and fled. There was a near miss when I spotted the "Cool Stuff" strategically planted by the door. I was completely transfixed until I asked the price—$123 per skein. While I really like this yarn, I cannot bear the look on the children's faces when we are all homeless (with fabulous sweaters) because I've spent the mortgage money on yarn. Weeping, we journeyed on.

As the yarn shop trip had been rough, we made the decision to stop at the Patons yarn outlet for comfort. We bought a little

Ballybrae and a few other things (okay, okay, okay, seventy skeins of yarn—it was on sale), stuffed it and my increasingly obnoxious children back into the car, and moved along.

The last stop on the yarn hunt was the far-flung yarn shop that I'd never been to. Ken and I arrived feeling pretty stress-ridden. The girls (ten, seven, and five) had lost it in the car, and Ken and I had been reduced to singing at the top of our lungs to distract them (or drown them out). We arrived at the last yarn shop ten minutes before closing. Now, for reasons I don't completely understand (ha!), two desperate, stress-ridden knitters with three berserk children, arriving at ten minutes to closing on a Saturday, is apparently not one of these ladies' favorite things. The plan was that Ken would purchase the dark gray, while I had a quick look-see for the yarn for a hat. This would be quick and efficient, and we would be out of there in minutes to take the three hot, tired, and crazed children home.

This was not what happened. What did happen was that my darling daughters, sensing that we were already not terribly welcome in this yarn shop, decided that they had nothing to lose and (this may be an understatement) lost their freaking minds. Ken and I took turns restraining them, and we beat it out of there in a dismal twenty minutes. I don't think we can go back to this yarn shop. Although if the ladies who were there that day are reading this (I'm sure you remember us) I would like to beg forgiveness on the grounds that no child can be nice about three yarn stores in three hours.

In the car we examined our finds, bribing the children with chocolate to get two minutes of peace. It turns out that we finally caught a break on the sweaters—the dye lots from the two different yarn stores actually matched. I almost cried from relief. I had worked out how Ken could combine two dye lots, but three made me feel slightly ill. How did we do it? Ken frogged the sleeve (want to see a grown man cry?) and worked the sleeves alternating the dye lots every two rows. Then the gods smiled again, giving him a full ball of the original left over to do the neck.

I learned several things during this period.

1. The limit on yarn stores for my children in one day is two.
2. Never buy yarn if there is no more, and you have only the exact amount you think you need (this is begging the knitting gods to take a shot at you).
3. My friend is a man of remarkable patience and good humor.
4. Famous designers are only human.

May 25
Unexpected Development.

I am very worried. This afternoon I decided to begin making up Ken's wedding sweater. His making up is atrocious, and after all we've been through with this, it just didn't seem right to have shoddy sewing. I rented the new Rugrats video for the wee ones and sat myself down for the task. Now, Ms. Designer wants me to sew the sleeves to the body, then block it, then sew the rest. Me, I *always* do as I'm told (stop that laughing!), and so I cheerily did the sewing and marched up to the bathtub to wash it. I thought about just dampening it, but as you will recall, this sweater has been knit all over Toronto, and is bound to be a little grubby. I washed it, squashed the water out in between towels, and strutted proudly downstairs to lay it out.

This is where it gets ugly. If you have a weak heart, then don't read on.

Try to imagine this: As I picked up the wet sweater, it grew. It stretched like taffy, in fact. It expanded more than six inches in length. It seemed to have grown some in width too, but the room was spinning around me too fast for me to get an actual measurement. Ken was off on a business trip, thank God, and wouldn't be over to see how it was going until tomorrow at six-thirty. Probably best, since this would likely finish him. When I spoke with him on the phone, somewhat later, I downplayed my own concern, but he felt that he needed two shots of scotch nonetheless.

I've pushed the sweater into the right measurements, but I'm concerned that when I pick it up in the morning it's going to grow right back out again. I've considered leaving it there, waiting until Ken gets here, then when he picks it up I can look astonished, and say, "What did you do?" He's new at this; I could probably convince him that it's all his fault. This is a last-ditch measure though, as the man is a dear friend and I really don't want to go on without him.

This is the first time that I've ever had this happen to a sweater. What went wrong? Will it be okay when it's dry? I need a plan if it isn't. Has anybody ever shrunk a sweater on purpose? Can you shrink superwash? Will all the stitch definition be lost? Oh my . . . I'm getting dizzy again.

I'm going to go have a little lie-down now.

May 26
Help, Whimper, Gasp.

This is it. This is bad . . . no, worse than bad . . . are there words for how bad this is? Ken's wedding sweater is still huge. I don't know what's wrong with it, but it's starting to look like this sweater that he killed himself over is one big unwearable disaster.

The length is now measuring close to three feet when I pick it up. The width is similar, if not greater, with the sleeves close to the floor. The texture is similar to lace.

Remember . . . this sweater was the right size when it hit the water. I measured it. The wedding is in a month. There is no way on earth that Ken can reknit it by then . . . if I do the lion's share we *might* make it.

Someone has suggested that putting it in the dryer might restore its original shape . . . I put it in for a few minutes, but frankly I'm terrified that I'm going to shrink it, and that then I won't be able to rip it back, if we end up trapped in the night-mare of reknitting it. I need help. What to do?

This is nauseating. I am eventually going to have to tell Ken (sometime before he sees it at six-thirty) what is up with this thing, and I'd like to have a plan in force to prevent him from running screaming into the street. The sight of this mess is enough to send a seasoned knitter into a catatonic state; as it is his first sweater, I expect his reaction to reduce him to the fetal position, gibbering and weeping. This sweater is cursed, plain and simple. I'm sure that this part isn't the designer's fault (since the one I'm knitting to match is fine) but I'm angry with her anyway. If you give me time

I'm sure that I can work out exactly how this is her fault . . . or maybe I could blame my mother . . . better yet, Ken's mother. I'm supposed to be Ken's knitting sensei, and look at this mess. I have no idea what to do. Some insane voice in the back of my head is insisting that I can frog it and reknit it before he gets here. Yeah . . . that's it, I can knit a whole sweater in seven hours . . . sure . . . I can do it. Ken will never have to know.

May 27
Bravely Going On.

The war wages on.

I have learned something about superwash wool, which I never work with because I don't like the feel of it. I have learned that the yarn is slippery, which is why it won't felt. My friends have told me that superwash wool is supposed to be tumble-dried; in fact, it often requires tumble drying. This is not, however, what the ball band says; the label says DO NOT TUMBLE DRY. Who am I going to trust, the collective wisdom of many knitters or the manufacturer? I throw the sweater in the dryer, checking it every thirty seconds. It does shrink down, not to its original dimensions, but at least to something smaller than an XXXXXL.

Looking at the label, I swing back and forth between two possibilities: First, that there was an honest mistake on the label, something that was lost in translation, or second, (this is the one I prefer) that the makers of this yarn are just plain vicious, and spend their days laughing about the poor helpless souls like Ken and myself, reduced to tears and scotch by their *not*-funny joke.

I remeasure the sweater after its brave journey into the dryer and back. Nuts. It's still too big. I'm suspecting Ken's tension was off, but can't figure how. He was knitting to gauge all along, and the sweater was handled plenty before this happened, so you would think that it would have grown (at least a little—just to hint at the disaster lurking ahead). Somebody mentioned that superwash wool should be knit a little tighter because of this whole "not sticking" deal. Perhaps that's the problem.

Ken's sweater is wider than it is long at this point . . . and it's plenty long. I've come up with the following plan. My willingness to execute this plan is an indicator of how much I love him, and so I've told him. I will:

1. Undo the shoulder seams (a thousand curses . . . my seams were beautiful).
2. Rip back the neck and the shoulder straps.
3. Rip back each and every piece of the sweater by one pattern repeat (this means that the sleeves will lose some of their increases . . . an added bonus) and reknit the neck opening to make it smaller.
4. Somehow make it less wide, by taking a rather astonishing three or four inches off each side of the front and back. (I'm telling you, this puppy is big. The shoulder seam sits at my elbow. It needs this much shrinking to *become* an oversize sweater.)

This last one is the killer. I know that cut-and-sew is probably what you are all going to suggest. I have some concerns about that. (Ha! Concerns! Obsessive, neurotic, quaking phobias are more like it!) My concern is that the same quality that makes the superwash all stretchy when wet—this slipperiness—is going to mean that it's likely to unravel. Part of what makes cut-and-sew with ordinary wool not so scary is that the wool holds onto itself. This (insert expletive of your choice here) yarn is not going to do this . . . right? So what if I sew, serge, whatever, down the sides and I miss one little strand and the whole thing just . . . well . . . imagine the horror! Ken and I would never recover. Professional help, that's what we'd need. Our friend Lene estimates that electroshock therapy might be a start.

For those of you concerned about Ken's mental health, know that he's taking this rather well. I called him at work a couple of times to prepare him. This was a really good move, since, by the time he saw it, it had made its trip to the dryer and wasn't as bad as he had imagined. He's currently kicking himself for coming up with this idea in the first place. Admittedly, while I'm sure that this will work out, a gravy boat does seem like a better wedding present than matching sweaters at the moment.

Here's the astonishing thing: Wouldn't you think that, given the litany of terrors this sweater has unleashed upon Ken, it would be years—perhaps never!—before he'd consider knitting another of these? Guess again. The brave and dear man currently has the exact same sweater on needles (in another yarn, thank heavens) and is attempting to finish it in a month in case the whole repair process on the first one doesn't work out. He's completely deluded, of course, but it seems to be giving him hope. Imagine trying again. It's a wonder he's sober, never mind knitting.

June 1
Where Do We Get the Strength?

It's been a harrowing weekend here. Ken and I finally accepted that cut-and-sew was our only option for narrowing the sweater. I lack words for the kind of terror that statement inspired in me. Three little words . . . and all I could see was this sweater unraveling from the cut sides into a wad of wool that resembled those freaky snack noodles that come in bricks.

Some of the reassurances from other knitters have not been confidence-inspiring. One knitter told me to be sure and run two rows of stitching as this "helps keep it from unraveling." *Helps*???!!!??? Oh Lord! The room spun around me. In a fit of neurotic panic, I decided not only to run two rows of stitching one stitch apart, but also to serge down the side. (The serger would bind the edge as it cut the extra knitting off.) Overkill, you say? I think not.

The die was cast: Mine would be the hand of death. I sat at the sewing machine and launched in. I used twenty-two stitches to the inch—don't laugh, I was freaking!—and ran down the sides twice. That done, I took out the serger, threaded the temperamental thing, and raised the sweater. Suddenly, with no warning, I lost it. A fit of nervous laughter overcame me. Ken, hovering and looking pale, announced a sudden need for the bathroom and took off. Abandoned, I began. After the first harrowing few inches, I calmed somewhat. The sweater was not unraveling into one big unrecognizable mess, and the edge looked okay. "Hey!" think I, "This isn't so bad." A wave of relief washed over me. Ken returned. He paled when he saw the scrambled mess that the serger was cutting off, but rallied somewhat.

Apparently, we got comfortable too soon. Just when I was on the brink of relaxing right into it—well, relaxing as much as one can while slicing up a sweater that took three months of Ken's life—disaster struck. The serger, for reasons known only to itself, decided to stop binding the edge but continued to cut. In essence it became a sweater cutter, not a serger. Imagine this for a minute. I'm serging away (or so I think), carefully watching the knitting going into the serger—I want it to be neat after all—when suddenly I happen to glance at what is coming out of the serger. A SLICED AND UNRAVELING SWEATER, that's what. It did not occur to me that it wasn't going to unravel very far, not with those two other rows of stitching, but I didn't think of this while all the air was going out of the room. Stunned, I began to gasp. I might have moaned. I'm not sure. What is sure is that I made enough noise to bring Ken from the other room. He came in slowly. I can only imagine what the dear heart was thinking, but he couldn't have imagined how bad it was.

At this point, I'm a little shaky on the details. I tried to reserge over the edge, but the serger had stopped trying and I was losing it. I began to cry, and to laugh hysterically (when overwrought I tend to combine the two); Ken retired to the bathroom again, where he admits that he may have shed a few manly tears. Once the crying had stopped, and Ken and I had gathered ourselves (we are apparently people of great bravery and fortitude), Ken took a turn at the serger. He didn't get it working, but we did divine the problem: Something just wasn't hooking up right. So we hooked in manually and were back in business. I fed it in the front, and Ken hovered above, watching the back to make sure that it didn't quit serging again. You have never seen two people more intense and intent in your life. The rather trying escapade wrapped up at two in the morning.

Ken is in the process of knitting the shoulder straps back in, then redoing the neck (on smaller needles); then I'll start back in with the making up. The wedding is looming before us. Hope we make it. If there is one more problem with these sweaters, I feel that I would be perfectly justified in throwing both of us upon a stack of 2-millimeter double-pointed needles and hoping for a fatal puncture wound.

Back to knitting the bride's sweater for me.

June 22
Finale.

Oh joy, oh bliss, oh blessed, blessed day. The wedding sweaters are finished. Oh, that felt so good I'm going to type it again. The wedding sweaters are finished. Yup, even better the second time.

I think I'm just going to wander through my day today, uttering the magic words over, and over again. I'm going to tell people who don't care. I'm going to tell the bus driver. I'm thinking about calling the yarn shop and everyone I ever met, starting with the *As* in my personal phone book, and working on through.

THE WEDDING SWEATERS ARE FINISHED.
THE WEDDING SWEATERS ARE FINISHED.
THE WEDDING SWEATERS ARE FINISHED.

The Cardigan Letter

$\mathcal{I}$ think I have a little problem. This morning when I came down from the bedroom I found this note skewered to a half-finished cardigan I've been neglecting. I'm trying not to be to alarmed, both because I have deep concerns about what would happen to me if my knits-in-progress did turn on me (I'm a little outnumbered, and they have all those pointy sticks) and because the note was held in place with an especially pointy blood-red metal knitting needle.

Dear Tramping, Harloting Trollop,

I've been there for you for almost four years, ever since the spring of 2000. I remember how it was in our salad days, back then in the beginning. You were charmed by me, you cast me on the moment you saw my well-written pattern and clear charts. We spent many evenings together, you and I, with you running my soft fibers through your hands, caressing my defined stitches . . . I thought we would be together forever. Perhaps I was naïve, but when you knit my whole back, both fronts, and a sleeve, I thought you were showing me real commitment. Now I wonder if it was all a lie.

When it started, it was just the small things, a sock, a pair of mittens. It was easy to overlook your duplicity, the way you were knitting other things. Everyone makes mistakes. I pretended not to notice that your mother had a new hat. Then it started to be embarrassing. Whole sweaters, several of them. A shawl—for crying out loud Steph, you didn't think I would notice a whole shawl? What did you think the other wool in the closet would say? I'm a tolerant project, but every stitch pattern has its limits and I wonder if you think I'm just supposed to let that 50 percent alpaca talk to me like that? I'm about ten seconds away from tangling his skein.

How long has it been since you said my name? You just laugh, sitting there with your self-patterning sock yarn, calling me The Sweater That Will Not Be Named. I know you think it's funny to put me down like that, but don't you think it hurts me? How do you think I feel when you put me in the basket and take out some cheap novelty yarn? "Alison needs a scarf"—yeah, sure. Everyone knows that hussy you're doing yarn overs with is 100 percent polyester.

Can't you see what you are doing? You will never find another yarn like me, I'm a discontinued line, and here you just turn your back on me? Why don't you just pull the needles right out of me?

This doesn't make any sense to me. You keep talking about how cold you are—look at yourself, sitting there in a cheap, common Wal-Mart cardigan with holes in it. Can't you see how you're hurting us both?

Do you think that I didn't see you with that lace weight last night? The swatch is right on the table. You don't even try to hide your wicked ways any longer. This has got to stop.

Just finish my sleeve and collar and do the making up, and we can be together, baby, I can keep you warm. I love you despite it all.

Ever thine, but running out of patience,
Your Cardigan

P.S. Touch the lace weight again and the alpaca gets it.

My response:

Dear Cardigan,

As soon as I was done sewing up your seams I could see what you were trying to tell me. Please forgive me for the three and a half years (four was a bit of an exaggeration, darling) that I neglected you. I was so wrong to stuff you into the knitting basket. I understand now that my normal urge to see other knits went too far. I could see that it hurt you, but I was selfish and I thought I wanted all that imported wool. I find their accents so charming that I forgot what a nice Canadian wool I had at home. Please forgive me for forgetting all of the reasons that we made this commitment in the first place.

I'm sorry for teasing you by taking you out of the closet and working three rows on you every couple of months. I see now that I was causing you pain, and I know I was leading you on. For that, I owe you a sincere apology. I know that you took my advances as signs that I was ready to come back to you; I should have been clearer about my emotional reluctance. I was knitting mohair, and it makes my concepts fuzzy.

I'm especially sorry for thinking that putting you inside the clear plastic zipper bag that the duvet came in was a nice way to keep the *dust off you. I realize now that I was only accentuating your loneliness by forcing you to view the world through a rippled, clear prison.*

Now that you have your strong ribs around my shoulders I never want to be without you. While I may wear other sweaters some days, know that my heart is always with you.

Stephanie

P.S. Even though I've sewn the buttons on lots of other stuff, with you it was really special.

The Thing About Socks

The thing about socks is—well, I'm not really sure what it is. I have knit hundreds of pairs of socks and I know hundreds of knitters who have done the same. Despite the seeming monotony of turning out all of these thousands of pairs of socks, not one of us is bored. Investing in sock yarn companies has continued to be a wise financial decision. There's something about socks that's special.

It could be because they are so portable. Dedicated sock knitters love the way you can tuck a sock into your bag no matter where you're going. A sock, no matter how close to completion, never becomes unwieldy or enormous or spills off your lap onto the floor of the waiting room or muddy bottom of the bus.

It could be because socks are so practical. Shawls are for special occasions; sweaters for cold days when they match your outfit; hats, scarves, and mittens are destined to stand between us and weather—but socks? Socks are everyday usefulness. Everybody needs them, from newborns to centenarians. A commonplace pair of handknit socks meets the human gold standard for belongings, being both beautiful and useful.

It could be because of socks' enormous variety. You can make cable socks, plain socks, socks with ribbing that goes all the way to the toes. Socks with intarsia, socks with Fair Isle bands, socks in intricate lace from top to toe. Get silk sock yarn, sock yarn that knits up all by itself into fetching patterns, sock yarn with mohair, or nylon or cotton. Feeling tired of tiny needles? Make boot socks from worsted weight handspun. Make tiny ankle high shorties or make a commitment, dammit, and knit a pair of knee-high kilt hose for your favorite kilt-wearing darling.

It could be because socks are cheap. Not as cheap as picking up five pairs for $10 at your local discount store, but cheaper than sweaters or afghans or scarves. A pair of socks takes only a skein or two, a finished project with a minimum of yarn investment. You don't have to save up for months to buy the materials and even an outrageous sock yarn stash can fit in the most modest of closets. (You might not be able to get anything else in there, but the stash will fit.)

Or it could be because socks are so intimate. Socks go on over bare skin, the only thing between the feet of your heart and the big cold world. Your rounds of stitches cradle the recipient's feet on their journey over the planet. Socks protect sensitive toes from cold floors and wrap them cozy before bedtime.

These are all really good reasons to knit socks, but they aren't the reason I knit them. I knit them because they are an unmistakable expression of love, simply because they do not last forever.

Used as it is intended, a sweater can be with you your whole life. Knitted blankets are passed down as heirlooms and sweet tiny baby things you make for your own little ones can be tucked away until your babies have babies of their own. Not socks. Used as intended, even with careful handwashing and conscientious care, a pair of socks has a lifespan. They can, of course, be darned. (I use my mother's method: I hold the holey sock over the garbage bin and loudly exclaim, "Darn it," before dropping it in. I'm a knitter, not a sock repair person.) Socks can be humored, but in the end—which isn't very far off, let me tell you—socks will be walked through. You can get reinforcing thread; you can knit in woolly nylon; you can carefully work a double thickness into the heel or toe, but socks are doomed.

This means that there's a lot of love in a pair of socks. The first one is a triumph of knitterly cleverness. The knitter casts on the right number, not so many that the socks fall down, not so few that they cut off circulation and turn your toes blue; then he or she works ribbing or picot or something to keep them from puddling unattractively around the ankles. There's the jaunt down the leg, perhaps with entertaining experiments in Fair Isle or cabling or lace panels. The heel flap, solid and practical—and then that miracle, the cunning three-dimensional heel (far simpler than it looks). The knitter picks up stitches for the gussets and then cruises down the foot (note: Marry small-footed persons), decreasing for the toe and grafting it shut, since the best socks are seamless. Feel the love? You should, since the sock knitter is only halfway there. The second sock of a pair becomes a deeply personal testament to stick-to-it-iveness as the knitter conquers the dreaded second-sock syndrome, surmounting the urge to cast on something new and exciting, something that doesn't come in boring, lackluster twos. When it is all over, when the socks are done, a knitter will have invested an average of twenty thousand stitches in the name of love and warm feet, knowing full well that the socks will wear out.

The knitter then gives the finished socks to a worthy recipient, who will, the first time that he or she puts them on, undergo a transformation, a moment of sacred joy, swearing off machine-made socks forever. And then—in a celebration of the knitter's art, a festivity of yarn, an homage to knitting in the round and needleworkers everywhere—the recipient will walk big honkin' holes in them.

That's love. That's why socks are special.

The Sheep Shawl

*I*n general, I am a process, rather than a product, knitter. I like the feel of the wool, the smell of the wool, the ritual of sorting through patterns, choosing the right needles, and casting on. (This could explain a thing or two about the number of unfinished objects in the house.) I like the moment when the yarn tells you what it would like to be. I like getting past the first little bit of the knitting, to the point when I can see the pattern develop and start getting a sense of what I'm making. I like how much knitting is like a magic trick. You have string and sticks; you wave your hands about, and there you have it—a sweater, a sock, warm mittens, a blanket, a shawl. I admit that it can be slow magic. Sometimes you have to wave your hands around for a really, really long time.

Being a process knitter, I'm not often really attached to the finished product. I give away almost all of my knitting and seldom knit for myself. My darling wears only handknit socks. I wear socks bought at the local mall. He sports a pretty fancy Aran sweater that I designed just for him. I slog about in a pathetically shabby store-bought cotton cardigan with a fraying sleeve that would give any "product" knitter the heebie-jeebies. I'm happy to give up any knitted thing. I had the pleasure of knitting it. I have a brief wave of knitterly pride when I finish it and I might go around the house for a day or two showing it off, but then I'm on to the next thing.

I even manage to feel pretty humble about my knitting most of the time. There are millions and millions of knitters in the world, and in other countries the most intricate and lovely things are made by mere children. I usually feel as if I've got no right to be particularly proud of the things that I make. Anybody could do it, if they knew how.

That might have all changed today.

I've been knitting the sheep shawl. It is my first large-scale excursion into lace. I've knit baby blankets and scarves of lace, but this is the big time. My mum (despite her complete loathing of knitting) loves sheep, and it's become a Christmas tradition for somebody to give her something sheep-ish each year. (I am pretty sure that this stopped being fun for my mum about five years ago, when the living room became fully saturated with sheep paraphernalia, but a tradition is a tradition, and besides, shawls are useful.)

It began while I was on vacation in Ottawa. Trolling through a local yarn store, I saw a pattern for the sheep shawl. Being sharp as a tack, I quickly grasped that this shawl could fulfill my sheepy obligations. It was a beautiful triangular shawl. Well-placed yarn overs and knit-two-togethers formed the delicate outlines of sheep cavorting in a meadow. It had a delicate pointy edging, and the whole thing was an heirloom. I decided that I could ignore my self-imposed yarn fast (besides, that's a yarn fast, not a pattern fast) and buy the pattern. I did not buy the yarn to knit it, being sure I could find something in the stash. (We will conveniently forget the fact that I looked for yarn but didn't see anything appropriate. Otherwise, I lose points for self-restraint.) Since the pattern was so reasonably priced, I also bought some other stuff because it's irresponsible to incur a debit card service charge for just one pattern. Right?

Three days later I was a little bit lost in Ottawa's rural hinterlands when I stumbled across a sheep/llama/alpaca farm. Like a creature possessed, I turned helplessly into the driveway. Where there are that many fiber-bearing animals, there will be fiber for sale. At the top of the driveway I found an older lady knitting socks in what was originally the garage but had inexplicably turned into a yarn shop, if rather an unconventional one. As fate would have it, sitting right on the table in front of me was a truly lovely dirt-cheap lace-weight alpaca, in exactly the right amount for the sheep shawl.

I wrestled briefly with the implications of it all—with buying yarn when I was officially on a yarn fast, using my family's vacation money for yarn (not that I hadn't done *that* before), and, most important, knitting the sheep shawl out of alpaca. But I decided it was just so clear. It was fated. Look at how it all fit together: I needed some new lace weight; I was lost in the boonies; I found yarn I could afford for the pattern I was planning—in a garage yarn shop? This was a no-brainer. I snatched the yarn up, paid in cash so as not to leave a paper trail, and raced back to my uncle's farm (where we were staying) to cast on.

At first I struggled with the way the pattern was turning out. This being my first real lace pattern, I was shocked by how it looked. This was not the elegant gossamer thing in the photo. This looked like a pot scrubber knit from dental floss. It seemed too strange and "open." I know now that knitting this—well— thread on largish needles is part of what makes the lace so fine and elegant, but at first all I could think was that I should go down one needle size, or maybe twelve. I struggled on, trying to believe that it's got to be in the blocking.

This shawl took perseverance. The lace-point edging went on until I was bleary-eyed, and the i-cord edging along the top was like walking on hot coals. Casting off did nothing to take away the pot-scrubber image. I started to worry that I might have spent all those painstaking hours knitting something that only resembles a shawl in my imagination. This thing looked like an alpaca version of those oriental noodles that come in weird bricks, four for a dollar.

I was not happy.

Then I blocked it.

Why did no one tell me about blocking lace? This was easily the coolest thing that I had ever done. I soaked the shawl in the bath, then spread its still-ratty-looking folds on the floor. Ever so carefully I stretched it out, gingerly pinning down each edge, each point, each wee cavorting sheep. Two hundred and eleven pins later, the curdled mass opened out into the most elegant, delicate, remarkable shawl. I felt like a hero. I felt like a knitting genius. I stroked it lovingly as it lay pinned to the carpet in the living room. I wanted to leave it there forever, so that all who saw it might know the joy that I felt at this instant. This shawl was my magnum opus. I was so impressed with myself that I had to go for a little walk to keep myself from unpinning it before it dried.

When it was actually dry, I found that I was, in reality, feeling a little nervous about taking out these strategically placed pins. What if it reverted to the Chinese noodle state when I picked it up? Maybe I hadn't done the magic right. I finally decided that it was best to unpin it right then, while no one was home. Then if it didn't work I wouldn't have to show it to anyone. I could just make up some story about a big bird getting into the house— yeah, that's it, a big bird swept down into the living room. I tried to fight it off with a knitting needle but it was too big and too angry. I was desperate; I fought for what seemed like hours, but I couldn't stop it from taking the shawl. I'll tell people that I'm devastated about losing it, but at least I escaped with my life.

Alibi in place, I unpinned the shawl.

It was still magic. It was a thing of beauty. It was . . . there are no words. I decided instantly that lace knitting is very, very, very cool. I also decided that I didn't want to give it away. My mother didn't know about the shawl. I could just keep it. I'd need to remember never to wear it in front of my mother, which might be a little difficult, given that I never wanted to wear anything else ever again.

Suddenly, in that very moment, I was no longer generous, or even a process knitter. It was all about the product and I wanted it to be *mine*.

I also experienced a remarkable wave of knitterly pride. I was no longer humble. I wanted to show people. I looked around. No people, and the cat wasn't impressed. I was alone.

I listened carefully; there were people on the street. Aha! My neighbors! Now I didn't know these neighbors very well, in fact, I didn't even know their names, but they seemed like nice folks. I was sure that they would want to see this shawl.

I didn't even stop to put on my shoes. I was on a high of rabid knitterly smugness. I rushed outside with my shawl, holding it aloft like the Olympic torch.

My neighbors looked surprised as I rushed up with this piece of knitting. Well, surprised might be a generous way of describing the look on their faces as I came bolting out of my house with knitting held aloft and ran excitedly down the street toward them, a barefoot crazy lady, yelling, "Hey! Hey, you! Want to see something really cool?"

They really were interested, and they asked me if I made it, and they gushed about how soft it was and said it sure was impressive, and wasn't I talented. Conceivably, they were thinking that it was safer to humor the nut ball with the knitting. But it made me feel good. I was prepared to believe that they meant every word.

I thanked them for their time, apologized for seeming crazy (they smiled and nodded, but they did think I was crazy), and I turned, temporarily pacified, to go back into the house to phone everyone that I knew to tell them that I was the best knitter in the world. I was a fine practitioner of this highly skilled art. I was proud to be a knitter.

As I walked away I heard my neighbor behind me as she said to her husband:

"Well, now, wasn't that some fancy crochet?"

The Entrelac Socks

Dear Famous Designer,

I'd like to apologize for all the things that I said about you last night. I was upset about my failure to accomplish your latest sock pattern, and I may have misdirected my anger. I know that there is no way that you heard what I said about you, but trust me . . . I owe you an apology.

When I cast on your entrelac socks (from your latest collection, AbFab Socks to Die For) I may not have had the best attitude. I'm sorry that I called the start to your sock "dumb-ass." It was really just that I thought that starting a sock with that little square and picking up stitches around it so that I got a round toe, was . . . well, I guess I owe you for the "colossal waste of time" crack too. I deeply regret that I did not trust that you might have a reason for making a toe that way, I'm sure that it's my fault that I don't have toes as round as yours. It's probably just a little birth defect. Now that I've knit a little ways on the entrelac part I see where you were going with that particular technique. It turns out that you aren't "out of your freaking mind," as I said you were. I guess I deserve the trouble I'm going to get into when I've got to work out how to position the heel, considering that it's pretty round too. You really did think it through. Sorry for doubting you.

After I so carelessly abandoned your toe structure for my own and got to the part where you knit the cute little triangles for the foundation of the entrelac, I'm afraid that I was perhaps a little rash when I said (sort of loudly) that you were "a few jalapeños short of a zippy salsa." It turns out that I misinterpreted an instruction that was actually very clear (if you are drunker than a wood louse in a rum barrel). Mea culpa.

Mostly, I feel that I must apologize for the . . . er . . . "episode" that I had when I got to the instruction for the first proper entrelac rectangles after the little triangles. After an hour of trying to follow the directions to knit one stinking little inane rectangle I may have said some things about you that were unladylike. (My husband, Joe, reminds me that my comment about you and "the horse you rode in on" was particularly callous. Sorry about that.) I eventually trashed your directions and did some other thing that worked out fine. I looked around online to try and find corrections or errata to your pattern but I didn't find any. Most likely that means that my problems with your instructions are my fault again, and that the tension headache and throbbing vein in my forehead are only what I deserve and not actually the end result of any substance abuse problems on your part, whatever I may have implied.

Finally, and with the most sincere of regrets, I have to take back every single nasty thing that I said about you and your pattern when I ripped the entire thing out at two in the morning and swore off entrelac, your pattern (regrettably), you yourself, and any children you may ever have. I was deeply, deeply wrong to curse your entire lineage. I must admit that I've discovered that I don't care for entrelac. Well, that's not entirely fair. While I may have said a thing or two about how I would rather have a root canal without anesthetic than entertain the prospect of knitting those crazy little squares again, what I really meant was that I don't like it in this application.

This is the only entrelac I've done, and it could be possible (as you imply, my dear designer) that it's more fun than sliding around naked in hand-painted merino (not that I would know) if you have the right project or perhaps the right instructions. It's not even that that I think entrelac is too time consuming or too hard. It's like this . . .

I'm not sure it's worth it. I've got no problem with "hard" knitting, designer darling, no problem at all. But if I'm going to spend a lot of time on something (read forty-seven hours of my life that that I will never get back), I want the damned payoff. These socks should be incredible. They are fussy and clever; the pattern must have taken hours and a degree in calculus to work out; and they should look like a million bucks. For the amount of time that they are taking, they should be so breathtaking that people would consider dedicating their lives to the pursuit of poetry, world peace, and a life of entrelac knitting worship when they see them.

Instead, I've managed to knit a dorky mess of freaky crooked squares that are no more beautiful than a five-year-old's first finger painting—and I'm not sure it's all my fault. I am now of the opinion that, having knit one half of one entrelac sock, I am the Entrelac Sock World Record holder. I know that your book has a shiny photo of a pair of finished entrelac socks, but with computer editing being what it is, I'm not convinced. Forgive me for not believing that anyone has ever successfully finished a pair, at least not using your pattern. No *offense intended, it's just that after my intense descent into knitting hell last night, I don't trust you as far as I could throw you.*

Therefore, my stalwart leader, my shining star, I have unceremoniously yanked the damn socks off the needles, (sorry for that crack about your mother), reclaimed the yarn, and moved on with my life. Furthermore, dear designer, I have forgiven you and once again must offer you my sincere apology for giving voice, however briefly, to the idea that you were "out of your everloving mind" when the inspiration for these socks came to you. The world needs visionaries, even ones who are clearly deeply delusional.

Thank you, and again, my deepest apologies—
Stephanie

two

Twenty Thousand Skeins Under the Bed:
Or, Stash and Why You Want It

The Beast

*H*eart pounding, pulse racing, fear coursing through my veins, I ran to the back door as fast as my legs would carry me. I reached for the knob, fearing that I'd be caught by the toothy beast in hot pursuit of me. I could hear its sharp claws on the pavement behind me as I opened the screen door and flung myself through it. I turned, stumbling, and slammed the door shut behind me. At last I was safe. Standing there, breathing hard, I was almost too afraid to turn and see if the thing had followed me. Nerving myself, drawing a shuddering breath, I made myself look out into my yard.

The squirrel was indeed there. Chittering angrily, it glared at me with beady little eyes and slowly backtracked to the patio table, where it stationed itself once again atop my freshly washed prize gray Shetland fleece. Again it started to stuff chunks of my beautiful fleece into its obscenely fat cheeks.

I'd had it with this squirrel. I'd been having trouble with it for two years. I try to be animal-friendly and environmentally cuddly, but I was starting to think thoughts about this squirrel that were anything but kind and gentle. I am a pacifist, a vegetarian, a tree-hugging ecofreak, but it's hard to maintain that gentle, responsible position when you're up against a predatory rodent with a spectacular attraction to your stash.

It started early in the previous summer on a lovely warm day. I had joyously hung a skein of finished homespun on the backyard fence to dry. Returning later that afternoon, I found my skein had vanished. Could a bird have carried it off? Not likely; it was a *big* skein. Considering that turkey vultures and albatross are virtually unheard of here in Toronto, there had to be another answer.

Maybe it had fallen over on my neighbor's side of the fence. No such luck. The skein was simply gone, vanished, disappeared. On one hand, I was deeply pissed off that my 190 yards of hard-won yarn—all those hours at my spinning wheel—had been taken from me. On the other hand, I found it rather charming that some furry city critter had so loved my wool that it had pilfered it to soften its home and prepare for winter.

I didn't know then what I knew now. Otherwise, charm wouldn't have come into it.

Over the course of that summer and the one that followed, said city critter stole, by skein and by handful, the equivalent of two full fleeces and about twenty skeins of yarn that I put out in the yard to dry. Now, I know what you're thinking. You're wondering, as any reasonable person would, why on earth I would have continued to put fleece and yarn into the yard once it had become obvious that the squirrel in question had both a wool fetish and an obsessive-compulsive disorder. I have no real answer, but several ideas. First, wool and fleece take several days to dry in the house but only a few hours in the bright sunshine. Toronto has a brief but cherished wool-drying season (some call it "summer") and the joy of sun-warmed, clean, dry fleece and wool is irresistible. Second, I am apparently just as determined as the squirrel. Many skeins and chunks of fleece were lost in failed attempts to safeguard the stuff. I tried boxes and tents and screens, hanging it on the clothesline—you name it, I gave it a whirl. I tried innumerable strategies to thwart the little stash rapist, each resulting in another missing treasure.

But now the squirrel had decided to take the question of wool ownership to the next level. I had carefully washed a treasured gray Shetland fleece and put it into the backyard to dry, using several bungee cords and an abandoned screen door as squirrel proofing. Because I love this fleece (and because you have to draw the line somewhere) I was also willing to employ surveillance. I had a cup of coffee, a nice chair, my knitting, and a pleasant day and I was going to sit in the late summer sunshine and watch fleece dry. The little fluffy-tailed rat wouldn't try anything with this sort of security. I was sure of it. The afternoon passed, the fleece dried, and all went well until sunset approached, and over the fence came the beady-eyed burglar.

I stomped my foot, banged my coffee cup, and scolded him with generally effective and helpful things like "shoo," "scat," and "git off with ya." He stared me down and I held my ground. I held it, that was, until the bastard (I have it on good authority that he was born out of wedlock) leapt from the fence onto the fleece, not more than a yard away from me, and screamed squirrel obscenities in my face. This scared the daylights out of me. I ran. I'm not proud of that.

Inside the house I pulled myself together and tried to figure out what to do. I laughed a little—imagine being frightened of a tiny little beast like that! Fortified, I opened the door to take another stab at fleece recovery, but the vicious little mammal advanced on me like I was out to defur him. For my own safety, I was forced to jump back into the house. There was no doubt in my mind that he had every intention of killing and eating me. He had the fleece, my beautiful fleece, and I was trapped in my own mudroom. I needed help.

My husband is useless at times like this. Yes, he can tell you at least one funny moose-hunting story and I have heard him give very solid advice on how to defend one's family from a bear, but smaller mammals are not his forte.

"Is it a gray one?" Joe asked, when I explained my plight. "God, I hate the gray ones." He barely suppressed a shudder. Joe is from Newfoundland, home of largish creatures, and he has made a poor adjustment to the smaller mammals Ontario is filthy with. Once when we were camping in Sandbanks Provincial Park (or as we like to call it "Sandbanks Provincial Raccoon Reserve"), Joe and I had, at four o'clock in the morning under the light of the moon, what is now politely referred to in our marital short-hand as "The Raccoon Fight." The raccoons were ripping our campsite up, stealing every scrap of food that we had, and Joe (despite my stern urgings) would not go and defend us from the bandits. The raccoon raid and our argument had ended with the now infamous line, "Get out of this tent and fight like a man."

If Joe won't defend food—our only food, I assure you—he certainly isn't going to do battle for a Shetland fleece. No, I was on my own.

I returned to the backyard to try again, only to discover that lifty lightfingers had evacuated, presumably to stash as much fleece as he could carry before returning for more. Quickly, I snatched up the damp fleece and brought it inside. Victory! He'd only gotten a pound or so.

The next morning, I couldn't let it go. My squirrel tolerance was at an all-time low. After complaining to anyone who would listen, and being referred by a friend of a friend, I found myself on the phone with one Frederick W. Schueler, Ph.D., curator of the Bishops Mills Natural History Centre and a heavy-duty wildlife dude. Fred had a couple of theories and a lot of information. I learned, for example, that squirrels subjected to overfeeding (as our antagonist surely was) become (and I quote Fred here) "deranged." Overfed squirrels apparently get cocky, overly brave, and develop a grotesquely inflated sense of self-esteem. Their inflated egos make them believe that they can take over an entire backyard, terrorize a family of five, and outwit a wily knitter determined to keep her fleece. (I am paraphrasing Fred here.) Furthermore, squirrels tend to be aggressive (no kidding, Fred—you don't say!) and the urban overfeeding only makes them more so. Overfed squirrels, Fred says, are insolent. I can confirm that, having been chased into my own mudroom by a furious wad of fantastically fast fur with murder in its eyes.

I pointed out to Fred that this whole wool fetish thing hadn't really come to a head with my hoarding small-pawed stash-stealer until I had put out the gray fleece. While he had stolen other things, and I'd learned a thing or two about his preferences (he doesn't take acrylic, likes wool, and is fond of alpaca but will not take qiviut . . . perhaps sensing that the arctic musk ox is too big for even him to take on), he has never actively defended a conquest before. Why now? Why scurry from the backyard when I pop out to retrieve a skein of white Corriedale or brown Romney, but go right to the wall for a gray Shetland?

"Gray?" asked Fred. Now there's something I hadn't thought of. Gray Shetland, gray squirrel. Perhaps his fascination was some instinct, some primitive urge to defend his like kind. Perhaps I had misread him. Perhaps his behavior was instead noble. Our little squirrel out there defending his young or a poor fallen fellow gray squirrel. Or perhaps (as Fred suggested) perhaps it is simpler. Perhaps the squirrel was responding to the most primitive of all calls to arms.

Perhaps . . . it's love.

Now that I could get behind. I could almost feel sympathetic. Imagine my furry foe, out there in the backyard, wracked with passion for his gray furry beloved while I try to drive them apart. Naturally he would fight me. (Let's forget for a moment that the romance of this beautiful interlude is totally wrecked by the part where he takes pawsful of his beloved and stuffs them into his cheeks. It spoils the mood.)

This brought us to the next point, however. What the hell was he doing with all this wool? "Nests," Fred assured me. I wasn't so sure. I reminded Fred that our little freakin' friend had two full fleeces (stolen a little at a time) and about twenty skeins of yarn in every color of the rainbow. Squirrels build nests in trees (Fred concurs) and that seems like a lot of fiber to take up a tree. Fred had told me that the home range or stomping ground of an urban gray squirrel is about an acre. I thought about that. If we used my home as the epicenter for the squirrel's turf, then there were thirteen trees close enough that they could house his nest. None of them was hollow, so if our wool-stealing buddy was . . . er . . . squirreling his stash up a tree, I would have seen it. Hell, my neighbors would have seen it. People would be talking about it. I would hear things on the street like "Hey, did you see that colossal multicolored squirrel nest down the street? I swear it's got pink mohair in it." It seemed unlikely. We needed another theory.

Fred, of course, had it. Sometimes squirrels will make use of holes or gaps in houses, building nests in the walls and attics of buildings. This made sense. I would expect that sort of good judgment from a beastie with the taste to get defensive about Shetland wool. He was clearly not a stupid animal. I looked out the window and gave it a thought. One acre: That's seven houses. Somewhere, likely all in one pile in one of these seven houses is all my wool and fleece. I wondered how I could find out which one. I toyed with the idea of knocking on the doors and quizzing my neighbors about surprising energy savings. Given wool's insulating qualities, it was entirely possible that in some nearby house, a husband was turning to his wife and saying, "Honey, doesn't the kitchen seem warmer this winter?"

There are, of course, ways to deal with animals that you don't get along with, but I'm an animal too, so I try to live with the local fauna. I understand that the reward for my tolerance may be to get ripped off by a deranged squirrel with megalomania, an urge to stash (which I can understand), and a torrid love affair with his kindred gray fleece. And so I asked Fred my last question.

"What's the average lifespan of an urban gray squirrel?"

Cracking the Whip

There have been some complaints from my family, or as I like to call them, TAKE (Team Against Knitting Enjoyment), that my yarn has been turning up in all possible nooks and crannies and attacking people with double-pointed needles bared. The last straw may have been when my husband, trying to put on a sweater he hadn't worn for a while, encountered a sock-in-progress stuffed down its sleeve. Don't look at me like that. The sock was originally perched atop a pile of other stuff in the sweater closet, but owing to a shortage of space it fell to the floor each time I opened the closet. Very annoying. Stuffing it down the sleeve of the sweater hanging there capitalized on unused space and made the closet tidier. You need to think outside of the box when you have yarn-control issues.

In my continuing attempt to live in harmony with these nonknitters I have decided to try and bring things under control a little bit. I'm going to clean out my knitting bags, my closets, my baskets, my freezer, and my bins in an attempt to consolidate my yarn collection. Note that I have given up attempting to reduce the stash—past forays into yarn nonproliferation strategies have proved to be folly. Mysteriously, such efforts only increase the stash. True stash reduction being a nonstarter, I have undertaken a condensation approach.

While corralling stash, I found some long-abandoned projects and I began tossing them in a pile. As the pile grew, an idea began to form. (My ideas should come with a warning. Some of the worst disasters of my life have been preceded by the thought, "Hey! You know what I should do?") My idea, before the whole thing got ugly, was that I should immediately vow to finish all these projects. I'd have a huge head start on Christmas, and it would feel good to have so many finished things. So far, most of these works-in-progress were more than half done; in fact, a lot of them were mostly done. I surveyed the pile. There weren't even that many of them.

That was it. I decided to make a commitment: *I, Stephanie, do hereby make a deadly serious promise to myself that I will not cast on any new project until I have dealt with (in whatever way I deem reasonable) all of my unfinished projects.* I was cracking the whip, I was getting it together. I was going to finish these projects and then I would be the kind of knitter who has one project at a time (maybe two, if circumstances demand it) and works on that one item until it's done. I'd always wanted to be that kind of knitter. Things seem to get done so quickly when you only have one project. (It is worth noting that I did not pause and reflect about why I have never been this kind of knitter . . . but self-examination is not for those in the grips of a new plan.)

I decided to go around the house and gather up all my projects.

I found two sweaters on the top shelf of the linen closet along with a scarf and mittens. The freezer yielded two shawls, a baby sweater, and socks (three pairs), and the empty space in the piano (Don't judge me—remember about thinking outside the box?) held a hat and scarf. One final check of my bedroom closet turned up an almost finished cardigan. I found two mysterious rows of ribbing on needles under the hair dryer in the bathroom. (I don't even know what those were going to be.)

I put all of these jilted projects on my bed. By now, it was quite a big pile . . . but never mind. I'd made a promise to myself and this time I was following through. Still scrounging around the house I found a wrap that only needed ends woven in and a baby sweater for a kid who was now in the third grade.

I kept looking for more forsaken projects, but it began to dawn on me that perhaps it wasn't in my own best interests to look *too* hard. The pile on my bed had reached epic proportions and was distracting me; I was beginning to find it daunting. I checked a couple more hiding spots and decided that I'd certainly found them all.

The pile on the bed now resembled what would be left behind if every member of an enormous and eclectic knitting guild was forced to evacuate the club's meeting place, taking nothing along. I began to take stock of the mountain.

I started adding up the unfinished projects. When I counted more than ten, I gave myself a stern talking to. How did I lose control like this? This tidying up would be good for me; it would be a self-imposed revolution. When the ruling class loses control and gets decadent, a revolution is just the ticket to restore balance. I simply never imagined that I would be the first against the wall when the revolution came.

When I got up to twenty knitting orphans, I started wondering what on earth motivated me to abandon these projects in the first place. Why did I do this to myself? There's that cotton intarsia sweater . . . I loved that sweater. Why did I put it down? Oh yeah, while I love wearing cotton intarsia sweaters, knitting them makes me feel like I'm getting meningitis.

I kept looking through the woolly deposit of projects. Now I'd counted more than thirty. Why didn't I finish this hat? I lost the pattern, that's why. Any reasonable woman would have given up and ripped it back, but did I? No, I saved it, because I believed that even though it had been years since I lost the pattern, it might yet turn up.

Still counting . . . thirty-five. These socks? I put them down because I was going to the movies and couldn't pick up stitches in the dark. I cast on another pair instead, completely forgetting these.

After careful assessment, I realized that the pile could be roughly divided into several subpiles.

Pile one: Good projects gone astray. Projects I adored that lost their place in the lineup because of my criminally short attention span. These projects deserved better. These projects were worthy.

Pile two: Projects of questionable worthiness. These were the ones where something clearly went wrong. They were missing patterns or yarn; they were knitted at the wrong gauge; they turned out to be as much fun as making your own toothbrushes out of the rough hair of a Persian camel. These, well. These I didn't know what to do about. A wise knitter would have reclaimed the yarn and tried again. I'm not a wise knitter, so I didn't have a plan yet.

Pile three: "I must have been drunk when I cast this on." This was stuff other people gave me, stuff that I bought because I fell for a 50-percent-off sale. Some acrylic that I started before I knew I liked wool better. Stuff with bobbles. Why did I start anything with bobbles? Bobbles were the work of some evil three-dimensional demon sent to vex me. I always thought I was going to conquer the bobble and I never did. Maybe if I wore a necklace of garlic while I was knitting bobbles . . . I hadn't quite figured out what to do with these either. Clearly, stuffing them into well-hidden locations around the house wasn't helping, although it probably did lower our heating bill.

By now, the pile was scaring the crap out of me. I was feeling as if I had personality traits that I didn't think of myself as possessing. This was the work-in-progress pile of a fickle, fickle woman. A heartless, spontaneous, wanton knitter who didn't mind trashing a project on a whim. A woman who cared nothing for staying power, getting things done, or following through. It was also the pile of a woman who apparently didn't think that there was anything wrong with buying as many knitting needles as it took to fill this urge, no matter how much this made her look like she had a porcupine fetish. Also (as I looked over the variety of things I had rejected or abandoned) I was either a person who really loved diversity or had a split personality. Wool, cotton, silk, lace, cables—I had forsaken them all at some point. I was clearly an equal-opportunity nonfinisher.

This was disappointing. All these were projects that at some moment in my past, I adored. For each and every one of them there was that magic moment when I loved it (or the idea of it) so much that I trashed everything else I was knitting. My knitterly heart may be fickle, but it's open. All of these yarns and projects were, at one time, my very favorite. They deserved more respect than this. Even the crappy acrylic could be better loved by another knitter than serving as box stuffing. The hat could be ripped back, reclaiming the yarn that I loved.

Okay, I told myself, I'm taking control. Today I tossed out a yarn catalog without even looking (much). I'm going to duct-tape shut my stash boxes and maybe put them in the attic with a drop cloth over them with some sort of electric field going on to try and make it harder to start new things. I am going to change my ways. I will begin with pile one today, and I will not cast on anything new until I've dealt with half of the total works in progress. I am freeing up space and opening the door to knitting hope again. I am not going to let the yarn down again. I will try to do better.

I had no idea I had so many size-four needles.

Nothing in My Stash

There is nothing in my stash. Despite my having . . . well . . . let's just leave it at a *lot* of yarn, nonetheless there is nothing to knit in my stash.

I'm a logical woman. I understand that I live on a planet with basic scientific laws about mass, space, and volume. I believe that these laws are true. If my stash really takes up this much space and yet contains nothing, there must be a black hole in my own home. Perhaps I should let NASA know about this.

I begin the delicate art of stash examination. I take my stash out of its boxes, its bins, its bags, its cupboards, its drawers, and its hidey-holes. When I have it all out, I come to two conclusions. As expected, I have a lot of yarn. As I suspected, there is nothing to knit in the stash.

I stand back, surveying the stash, and say aloud, "I have nothing to knit." This simple sentence gets my husband's immediate attention. "Sorry. *What* did you say?" The look on his face is beyond description. "You think you have no yarn?" He is clearly incredulous. I can see his point. A woman standing hip-deep in yarn who says she has nothing to knit might need some kind of professional help.

Here's how I explain it to him. Stash isn't just stash; it has distinct components that affect its knitability. My stash consists of the following:

1. Core stash. This is yarn that to be completely honest, I am likely never going to knit. It is discontinued yarn that is too rare to knit. It is yarn that is too expensive and is too special to knit, or it is yarn that is so beautiful that I am not worthy of it. In my Core Stash is some of the Patons Ballybrae that they don't make anymore in a color so perfect for me that when we met I knew it was kismet. There is Irish Aran wool, the real stuff, soft, thick, and perfectly cream. There is the lace-weight Shetland that is far better as an imaginary shawl; my real knitting could never match the shawls that I knit with my imagination every time I hold it. Core stash is the foundation of every good stash. It is inspiration. It is beautiful. It is the reason that I knit, but it is not for knitting.

2. Souvenir stash. If I look deep within my knitterly soul, I don't believe that I'm going to knit this either. The soft blue handspun that I found in a tiny shop in rural Newfoundland, the wool that I got in Hawaii (especially valuable because it may have been the *only* wool in Hawaii), the tweedy yarn my friend brought me from Scotland, the cotton from Italy. This is remembrance yarn. This yarn is

postcards of my life. Here are the leftovers from my first stranded sweater, the twelve colors from an intarsia sweater that was nothing short of a personal victory. With this yarn I can document every trip, baby, and yarn shop of my life. Who would knit that?

3. Sale stash. This is yarn I bought because I have a limited ability to walk away from a 50-percent-off sign, no matter how ugly, odd, or inexplicable the yarn. I'm never going to knit it. If I'm lucky I'll grow enough as a person to be able to donate it somewhere.

4. Transient stash. This is the only yarn that stands a chance of being knit. The transient stash is forever shrinking, not only because I knit it, but because it is very easily converted to other forms of stash. Firstly, transient stash can automatically convert to souvenir stash if it remains in the queue for too long. Buy some wool, stick it in the stash, don't get to it for five or six years, and then—Bam! I'm standing there with the wool in my hands saying "I remember when I bought this . . ." That yarn is thereafter not for knitting. Leave a lovely sock yarn in there for a decade or so, and it turns into core stash. Decide that I love it too much to decide? Done.

I feel sort of guilty about the stash sometimes. I feel especially bad when I'm in yarn shops buying more because I don't seem to have anything, even though I've got almost as much yarn as the shop itself. The thing is, I explain to my husband, it's not so bad. There are worse things to collect, like cats or bicycles or those creepy dummies that ventriloquists use. I pause for effect, allowing him to imagine a house covered in blank staring wooden comrades.

Really, when you think about it, yarn stash isn't that bad.

But I still have nothing to knit.

Mine, Mine, All Mine

*L*et's cut to the chase, shall we? I hoard yarn. It goes well beyond buying yarn on sale or putting away some particularly yummy yarn for the future. It even goes beyond the very common knitterly urge to collect far more yarn than I can ever knit in my lifetime.

Some knitters have the equivalent of a personalized yarn store in their house, and that's how they use it. When they consider a project, they "shop the stash." Others have a stash for inspiration; they cruise the stash combining colors, exploring textures, feeding the creative muse. Their stash is their palette.

I am not like these others. I must confess it.

The first hint of a problem emerged when I was teaching my kids to knit. My daughter asked me for a ball of yarn to make a hat. I love my daughter desperately and I have a generous stash, but when she refused the ball of truly ugly green acrylic that I offered her, I opted to take her to the yarn store and buy her some yarn instead of forking over a ball of my own. I went so far as to lie to her—er, I mean mislead her—about some yarn that she liked in the stash. I told her it was scratchy. (It was actually an Italian merino crepe. There is butter out there that is scratchier than this yarn.) I told myself that I wasn't being selfish; I just didn't want my good yarn ruined by a child who as yet lacked the knitting ability to make an object worthy of the yarn. I justified my decision still further by telling myself that even if she did manage to knit a nice hat, she would probably just lose it anyway. She's thirteen. She can't be trusted with stash yarn.

I did wonder if maybe I had a problem parting with stash when she accused me of only offering her the "crap yarn," but I ignored the twinge of insight. I'm sure that everything about my knitting habit is perfectly emotionally healthy.

My husband Joe asked for a sweater. I happily got my coat and credit card and started quizzing him on what kind of yarn he would like. I love him deeply, and I will gleefully part with time and money to make him happy. I babbled on about what kind of design it should be, how handsome he looks in cables, all the while getting ready to fling myself out the door into the snow, make my way across town in the cold, on the bus, to buy him some yarn. He told me I didn't have to go to the yarn store. I looked at him as if he had three eyes. How on earth can I knit him a sweater without buying yarn? Silly man! Confusion gave way to shock as he told me that he had been looking in the stash. (Did you hear that? *Looking in my stash.* Is nothing sacred?) He said that had seen a really nice yarn, and that there were twenty skeins of it, and that he wanted his sweater knit from that. I surprised even myself when I told him that it was absolutely out of the question. No way. I am not using that yarn for a sweater. I'm saving it. I don't want it to be gone. I want to be able to look at it when I open the stash; I want it in its skeins with the labels still on it. Mine, mine, all mine. He insisted. That was definitely the yarn he wanted. It was when I decided to go online to see if I could buy more of that same yarn that I realized that I might, just possibly, have stash issues.

My stash is remarkably static. Things go in, but they rarely come out. Now, not everything I buy goes into the stash, or at least not into core stash. I have an "outer ring" of stash. I buy it and it gets knit up pretty quickly and never makes it into the stash closet. True stash yarn goes into core stash and it never comes out. If I need yarn from core stash, I go buy something like it. Core stash is not there for using. It is there for "being." It is not yarn; it is a monument to knitting. It is my homage to wool. It is there to be admired, revered, and uncorrupted, and if Joe thinks he can mess with that, he's out of his mind.

Joe need never know. His yarn sense is not as finely honed as mine. I am certain that I can find yarn close enough to what he wants; as for my precious yarn, it can go deeper into core stash, where Joe will never find it. I will just make a little trip to the yarn store tomorrow, while he is at work. I'll pay cash so there's no paper trail. My darling can have his sweater, and I get to keep my yarn. Is this clever, or what?

Stash issues? I don't got no stinking stash issues. Nope, not me.

If You Have a Lot of Yarn . . .

$\mathcal{T}$he knitting newsletter comes to my mailbox four times a year, always full of patterns, suggestions, and stories about knitting. This spring, it had an article about storing and organizing your stash. The article had some really good suggestions, like arranging your yarn by weight and color and storing skeins of yarn artfully clipped to hanging chains where people can see and enjoy them.

These suggestions were great. When I had followed all of them, I had managed about 10 percent of my stash and had to stop. There are only so many chains of yarn you can hang in your home before you start blocking exits. Clearly, the author of the article and I are leading very, very different lives.

Perhaps part of the problem is that I'm a spinner as well as a knitter, so there is an ever-increasing mass of fiber that will become yarn and yarn that recently was fiber. Becoming a spinner has also cut into my knitting time while increasing the yarn stash, which increases the yarn supply at an alarming rate. It does not help that I live in a shoe box of a house, or that I'm sharing this house with four other people who seem to feel that they have a right to have some stuff stored too.

Perhaps it is that I buy yarn in a way that makes it clear that on some level I must fear that there will be no yarn for sale tomorrow, or that due to an evolutionary glitch attached to global warming, sheep will suddenly stop bearing fleece any minute now and my stash is the only thing that stands between me and the nightmare of knitting nothing but acrylic eyelash yarn for the rest of my life.

We will likely never know what the exact factors are that change a perfectly normal yarn stash—which can be handled by methods suggested by a thoughtful article in a newsletter—into something that has turned into a lifetime commitment. My stash does not need mere management. It needs to be beaten into submission.

Those who are competing at the extreme sport level of stash storage in small homes, and have obsessively managed to procure more yarn than could ever be knitted in ten lifetimes, need more help than a well-meaning newsletter can give. Not only do we need excessive amounts of storage space; it must be subtle. Stashing for retirement and beyond means that you may have so much yarn as to cause so-called "normal" people (if that's what you can call people with no yarn at all) to report you to mental health authorities.

Attempts should be made to keep extreme stashing discreet. After many years of cohabitating, my darling is still not sure exactly how much yarn I have. He knows it's a lot, but through innovative and daring yarn storage strategies, I've managed to keep the exact quantity secret. It's not as hard as it sounds, since I don't think that he really wants to know.

In my home I have an established yarn zone. This is where I pretend to keep my yarn. I do keep some yarn there, but my stash is like an iceberg; only the top 10 percent is visible. The rest of the stash lurks unseen and unknown, sunk deep below the surface of my Victorian semidetached. My smoke-screen long-term stash is more or less contained in the linen closet, stuffed into boxes, plastic containers, Ziplocs . . . whatever will get it in there. My short-term yarn and projects fit into enormous baskets in the living room. These portions of the stash are mostly organized in a way that would make a yarn organizer proud, though anyone who believes a stash should stop there may want to avert his or her eyes and skip to the next story in the book.

That other 90 percent is where extreme stashers need to get creative. If you have so much yarn that you are resorting to these measures then I'm pretty sure that discretion is in order. Not everyone understands. To help get you started, here are a few strategies that work for me:

1. The freezer. We have been vegetarians for quite some time. Vegetarians just don't need chest freezers. I didn't get rid of mine, it's still plugged in and running, and I'm certain that you can guess why. Yes, my fellow zealots, my freezer contains four pork chops from 1986, a loaf of bread (to justify the freezer), and my enchanting (if frosty) collection of Ballybrae that I scored when the Patons outlet closed. Freezers provide lots of potential space and offer the added bonus of being 100 percent mothproof. If you can give up meat, this will work especially well for you.

2. Closets. I know, I know—you're thinking that closets aren't discreet, that many knitters keep yarn in closets, and that if you had a closet to put more yarn in you wouldn't have a problem in the first place. Well, my skeptical fiber friend, you gotta think outside the box. Go to the store. Buy a suit bag, the kind that you hang in the closet. Black is good, but anything other than transparent works well. Now fill the suit bag with yarn. Try to stick with wool and acrylics. Cotton is too heavy for the bag; it will break the zipper and blow your cover. When you have the bag full, just hang it in the closet and admire how it just sits there looking like a suit. (Note: Should you forget the "no-cotton" rule and have a suit bag explode in your closet, spilling yarn into plain view and causing your family to stare at you incredulously, it is best to distract them. The moment they start looking at you like you should be in treatment, ask them very loudly who was screwing around with the zipper. Take enormous care to glare at them like it is their fault that a suit bag full of yarn has just exploded in your closet.) Got more yarn? Of course you do. Start stuffing. Yarn in skeins fits beautifully down the sleeves of suits and coats. Avoid stuffing the sleeves of your mate's clothes. I assure you that he or she will not think that this is either clever or normal behavior.

3. The piano. Not everybody is going to have this option, but my piano has a panel down by my legs that can be lifted out. It reveals a space that runs the whole width of the piano and goes from pedals to keyboard. Filling this space with yarn

does not change the sound of the piano in any way, assuming that you don't pack yarn right around the pedal cables. Remember to remove the yarn before the piano tuner comes. Piano tuners don't seem to understand yarn hoarding either.

4. Kitchen cupboards. How about those top cupboards? Could you fit some yarn into the canning pot that you only use for six jars of jam once every seven years? How about your gravy boat? A lone ball of silk fits in mine. Casseroles? The cookie tins you only use at Christmas? How about the Tupperware that you don't use at all? Get innovative—every little bit helps.

Think outside of the box. You'll need to, since all of your boxes are full of yarn anyway. Got a nook or a cranny? Stuff a little yarn in there. Trunk of the car? Cushions on the couch? Squirrel that yarn away and remember that with advancing years your memory will fail you, and finding your yarn again will become a pleasant surprise.

Be innovative; ignore those who think you mad, and for goodness' sake, if you think of somewhere good, drop me a line.

The System

Who says I don't have a system?

If you know me, then you know that as soon as the holidays come around, I become a trifle twitchy. Seeing a loved one wrapped in a really good sweater gives me a wonderful feeling. I have a tendency to get excited about wrapping everyone in this frosty climate in wool, and I overcommit to holiday gift knitting. I admit it: I tend to go over the top and cause myself a little stress.

By "a little stress" I mean that I actually end up with so much on the needles that by the time the presents are due, I'm a raving, sleepless, knitting maniac. I do this every year. I always swear that this year I'm going to cut back. This year I'm going to be reasonable. This year I'm not going to try to knit twenty-three pairs of gift socks in four days and then beat myself up for not managing to warp the space-time continuum to get it all done. I swear that I'm not going to spoil my holiday by depriving myself of seasonal fun while grafting sock toes at 4 A.M.

This year I have a plan for preventing the holiday meltdown: I am going to take advantage of all the half-done projects that I have ever accrued and finish them all up so that I have lots of presents in half the time. If I put these "head-start" projects into the queue with stuff that I'm already working on, it will be less of a commitment. It will both deal with tons of guilt-inducing space-occupying works-in-progress and thrill my family and friends with buckets of knitted things that are actually finished. It's the perfect plan. Feel free to try it yourself.

In order to execute this plan, I need to hunt up all of my projects and this means going into the stash. My stash is arranged in a format that resembles an archaeological dig. The most recent additions are near the top. Older yarn and projects emerge as I dig through the layers. Unlike more organized knitters, who have their stash put away by weight or color, mine is easily sorted into age layers. If I want something from four years ago, I know that I need to start a fair ways into the stash. Likewise, I know that if I want to find a neon-green oversized chunky-acrylic sweater with dolman sleeves that would put a flying squirrel to shame, I need only go down to the layer representing the early eighties.

To enhance the element of surprise in my holiday endeavor, I decide to start at the bottom (oldest) layer and work my way up. I know what I've abandoned recently, but I usually manage conveniently to "forget" anything that's been in the stash awhile. It may well be that I have so much stash that the newer acquisitions simply push the older stuff out of my memory. Every brain has its limits. I suppose there is also the chance that I don't *want* to remember much of it—for example, that neon-green flying squirrel sweater.

I pull out the top boxes, bins, and bags and work my way down to a plastic box that hasn't seen the light of day in years. I'm extraordinarily excited as I dump the box onto the bed. What could be in it? The suspense is killing me. I root around among the yarn until I find a cloth bag. The first of many unfinished objects! What will it be?

Briefly I allow myself to imagine what could be inside. A half-done sweater? Most of a scarf? A hat that only needs a seam? What treasure did I hide for myself? The possibilities boggle the mind. For the purposes of this experiment, I don't allow myself to consider that what is in the bag might have been abandoned for a reason—say, a pair of slippers knit out of that weird plastic yarn that everybody's strange Aunt Alma loves, or a foray into cotton intarsia kitty cats . . . It's better not to imagine what sort of knitting breakdown from my past I might uncover.

I decide that I want this moment of discovery to be perfect. I take the bag downstairs and snuggle into my knitting chair with a cup of coffee. My plan is all coming together.

I open the bag and empty it into my lap. It's a sock. A completely finished sock, along with the pattern I used, the needles and the yarn. A beautiful Fair Isle sock.

A familiar Fair Isle sock. *Really* familiar, in fact.

I look down at the knitting basket by my chair that holds my current projects and I quietly pull out another cloth bag. Unceremoniously I dump its contents onto my lap and a pattern, yarn, needles, and a single finished Fair Isle sock tumble into my lap.

I confirm my suspicions and feel only unmitigated joy as I hold the current sock and the years-old one together.

I have a pair.

This system is going to be great.

Moth

Knitters are, on the whole, lovely people. It is difficult to imagine that knitting could lend itself to hateful activity. I find it improbable that many knitters are plotting to overthrow governments or planning murder while knitting booties. The act of knitting and acts of violence seem so dissimilar that I like to believe that knitters are, without exception, kind and peaceful, without an adversary in the world. But I do recognize, for all our kindness and gentle ways, knitters have a natural enemy: *Tineola bisselliella,* the common clothes moth.

On the day that this story begins, I was poking around a yarn shop. As usual, I had far more time than money and I spent a lot of time investigating sale bins, diving into the depths of clearance boxes, and gleefully excavating the backs of displays. Brace yourself now, and if you have a weak stomach, turn back here.

I saw a moth. I also saw some little buggies of undisclosed identity lurking about in the bottom of a sales bin.

Despite the fact that I am a knitter and, therefore, discriminate against moths in a reflexively unfair way, I do try to mediate my response. Perhaps this is a little too granola for some knitters, but the way I see it, it's probably unrealistic to expect that there wouldn't be some critters who eat wool in a wool shop. It's an enormous buffet and the wool-eating infiltrators are only doing their thing. I'm sure that lots of yarn store owners wage war on moths on a regular basis. I can understand that this is apt to be a silent issue, and that no yarn store owner would ever admit to having a moth problem. It seems counterproductive for a yarn shop owner to make an announcement that would send her clientele screaming into the streets. But it only stands to reason that the occasional yarn store infestation happens. I figured that it was my responsibility to protect myself, so I didn't freak out. Peace and love.

I bought myself some dandy wool that wasn't anywhere near the winged pox (whose presence I completely respect as part of the circle of life) and left the store. I inspected the wool very carefully, and when I got home, I put it in quarantine, keeping it away from the main yarn stash until I was confident that it was "a clean hit." It was a good-looking wool with no sign of trouble.

That was a couple of months ago. Now, I confess, I probably should have microwaved it to kill any potential moth eggs or taken some sort of preventative action, but I didn't. I relied solely on the slightly riskier quarantine method. I know that this is disappointing to moth activists and I'll try to be a better person from now on, since considering what came next, I may have made an error in judgment there.

Scene 1

The kitchen. Enter knitter stage left. Cue moth to flutter near cupboards.

I saw a moth. In my home. Remember all my lovely sentiments about how the moths are just doing their thing? You know, we all the share the planet, you have to expect wool-eating critters where you have lots of wool? All that lovely talk about how if you have a yarn buffet, you can't really blame anyone for coming to dinner? Screw it. This moth was in *my house*. I froze in my tracks. I stared at the moth. (S)he didn't stare back. (S)he just fluttered about, trying to act all innocent and avoiding eye contact. I fell for it. The moth was in the kitchen. (S)he was probably a cereal moth, sure . . . that's it. That made sense. (The astute among you will note that this rationalization makes no sense. I have way more wool than cereal.) Even though I managed to believe that this was not the sort of moth that would eat my wool, I was uncomfortable with him or her and I delicately removed the moth to the backyard near the butterfly bush. Just to be safe, I gave the stash a cursory inspection, paying special attention to the bag of yarn from the yarn store with the moth problem. Nothing, *nada,* zip. Perfect stash. No indicators of any kind of beastie whatsoever. I resumed my kind critter-tolerant life.

Scene 2

Repeat Scene 1, only increase the level of alert and jumpiness of the knitter.

Scene 3
The kitchen. The knitter is making dinner, the moth aloofly flutters by the Brussels sprouts.

This time, I decided to check all my cupboards. (Yes, it does say something about the sort of housekeeper I am that I decided to do something about it on the third sighting.) I spent an hour looking for the infested cereal (because in my special world of denial these moths still had to be cereal moths). I found nothing, but did succeed in trashing my own kitchen and creating several hours of work for myself. I decided to throw away a bag of oatmeal and some cornmeal anyway. It made me feel like I was doing something.

Scene 4
The knitter is in her bedroom/office talking on the phone. Cue "cereal moth" to flutter through doorway and across computer screen.

When I first saw the moth-that-eats-cereal-and-not-wool in my office, I stopped to think: *Wait just a minute here. The office has no cereal.*

It took a few horrible seconds for the truth to sink in. There might be no cereal in the bedroom but it was, however, about ten feet away from *my stash*!!!! Without even a nod to the possible karmic implications of such an action, I squashed the living daylights out of the moth. I'm not sorry that I did either.

It was time. I could no longer ignore the possible threat to my stash. I ripped apart all of the stash boxes and inspected all of it to within an inch of its life. After hours of making a mess of it, I found nothing. No moths, no moth larvae . . . zip.

I used a few choice swear words that I need not share and checked my clothes. I checked the kids' clothes. I checked the out-of-season coats hanging in the downstairs closet. In a completely desperate move, I checked the bin of single socks in the laundry room.

The evidence continued to evade me. I began to think up questions:

1. Can there be moths if I can't find evidence?
2. Am I looking for the right kind of evidence? What is the evidence?
3. Can our suspicious little infiltrator simply be a moth from outside?
4. Assuming that he is not an interloper, but a visitor, what can I do to keep it that way? Is there a magic protection I can work on the stash?
5. If I can't find moths now, how do I know when they are dead?
6. Is it normal to feel this nauseous when the stash is threatened?

Clearly research was needed before I could relax. I got books from the library. I e-mailed other knitters. I called the government. (This last idea seemed more reasonable at the time. I thought somehow that they would know something. Doesn't it seem as if there would be a department of Canadian bug research or something? You would be surprised how little the government of this enormous country knows about the common clothes moth. You would probably not be surprised by how little they cared about my dilemma.) I spent hours learning a great deal about moths and their antiwool ways. The fact that I had no moths on which to inflict this knowledge did not deter me at all.

Scene 5
Several months in the future. The knitter appears happy and relaxed. There are no moths in sight, though it is clear that the knitter should dust the house.

I wasn't thinking about moths at all. In fact, now that some time had passed, I had almost forgotten about moths. I was no longer on high alert, since the variation on Murphy's Law regarding moths says that if you have spent days giving yourself a course in moth prevention, murder, and disposal, you will likely never see another moth. I had resumed my happy life and am a peaceful knitter once again.

One day, I went deep into the stash, far, far past the canopy, and dredged up a beautiful Aran I had put away a year before. I settled on the couch and put the balls of beautiful cream wool beside me. I began to knit, but I only got a few stitches along before I had to pick an odd little cobweb off the yarn. Strange, thought I, but I wasn't the sort of person who pays much attention to odd things, so I kept knitting. A few moments later, there was another. A weird little cocoon-shaped cobweb.

It took a minute. Then it started to hit me. Slowly.

Cocoon?

Remember the moths I couldn't find? Remember how there was no evidence? I spread the Aran on my lap and looked closely at it. The horror spread over me as I saw little holes and weak spots, cocoons, and in one spot an interloper that was almost too nightmarish to speak of, an actual moth larvae eating my sweater. He didn't look even the least little bit sorry or ashamed.

I immediately ran to the kitchen and shoved the sweater into a garbage bag. I didn't even stop and rescue the needles. I vacuumed the place where I'd been sitting, and then (despite my deep concern for the stash) I took a very, very long shower.

After hours of exhaustive legwork, inquiry, and investigation, things started looking up. Only the box that the sweater was in had any evidence of moths or of evil moth offspring or . . . well . . . seemed suspicious. I needed only two drinks to get through checking the entire stash.

I then developed a comprehensive plan for blasting the little nasties; one that, I think, was reasonable—although (I ask you) if vicious vermin were poised to eat all your yarn, what would you think was unreasonable?

The plan:

1. Positively identify the enemy. These were little beige moths with little brown heads. These were clothes moths. Their offspring were tiny little worms of the same coloring. These were the enemy! Don't feel sorry for them, and don't worry about the impact of killing them on your karma. They started it.

2. The whole stash went into the freezer. I live in Toronto, which was a freezer at present, so I stuffed my stash (which wouldn't fit in a freezer anyway) into garbage bags and tossed them into the backyard. For the sake of safety, I bagged and tossed all acrylics, even though moths find them unpalatable. I wasn't taking the chance that a moth could take refuge in there until I brought the wool back indoors. I also bagged and tossed all works in progress. I left them there for three days. The sweater and yarn at the epicenter of the attack stayed in the garbage, joined by everything else in that box. As much as the thought of throwing away all that work and wool made me deliriously hostile, it was better than letting down my guard and having the filthy winged beasts back.

3. After three days I brought the stuff in. Straightaway I began unbagging and sorting. I carefully inspected for any of the little cocoons, holes, or other evidence. Then I shook each skein or work in progress over a clear plastic drop cloth on the kitchen floor. Listen carefully—did you hear that sound? A noise like little bits of sand hitting the plastic? Those were eggs. Any yarn that made that noise was getting special attention.

   I made three piles: acrylics; wool or wool blends that didn't appear to have any evidence of infestation and weren't near anything that was infested; and stuff that showed evidence of infestation, or made sand-dropping noise over the plastic, or was in the same container with stuff that did.

4. Any yarn that made that noise got beaten half to death outside, then vacuumed. Some tight balls had to be skeined to do this really well.

5. I rebagged *everything,* even the acrylics. I kept it separated into the three groups. Moths were nasty enough not to be trusted. They might not be eating the acrylic, but they could be hiding in there. I left everything bagged up in a reasonably warm place for a couple of days. Then everything went back outside or into the freezer. The first freezing should have killed anything that was alive in the wool but didn't get the eggs. (When they come back inside, they think it's spring and hatch, and then you freeze the little bastards—sneaky, yes?) The sneakiness made me feel better.

6. After three days of freezing, I brought the bags in and repeated the beating, shaking, and vacuuming with the wool that was suspect or infested. I put the acrylics away and let the rest warm up in the bags for three days.

7. Anything that had absolutely no trace of moths could now be microwaved. Nuke the stuff for about ten seconds per ball. Watch the labels. I had one spectacular event because I missed a staple. (Don't do this—although if you have kids they will be really impressed.) It's also a good idea to do this alone in the house . . . some people just wouldn't understand.

8. The stuff that was infested took two more trips through the freeze-thaw-beat-vacuum cycle. (Do you want to win or not?)

9. After the freezing business, I microwaved, skeined, washed, and carefully dried the wool that was directly involved. I bagged it in a clear bag so I could monitor the bug situation. Remember: Moths are devious, underhanded little critters well equipped for survival. Don't let your guard down.

Given my unwillingness to use a chemical solution (sorry, but we're ecofriendly tree-hugger types), and the research I did, I didn't think that there could be any moths left after this. While the stash was making its trips in and out of the great outdoors, I also washed, vacuumed, and dusted every square inch of my house that had had wool in it. This was a big job (I think there is wool in every room of my house) but again, I decided to err on the side of caution.

I'm watching. Just you wait, you little horrors: Show a single wing and you are *toast*.

three

Dangerous Liaisons: Or,
Yarn Can Be Addictive

Archaeology

I'm knitting a sweater, and I think I've almost knit far enough that I could start the shaping for the armhole. It's a great moment, moving from one phase of a project to the next, meeting goals, and getting things done. You would think that I would be thrilled. You would think that I would be sitting with smug satisfaction, peacefully contemplating accomplishment and serenity. Instead, I am ripping up the living room.

I have pulled all the cushions from the couch. My baskets of projects and yarn are overturned and the contents scattered. Balls of yarn have rolled everywhere. The credenza that the TV sits on is opened and trashed, and I am in the process of dumping every single thing out of the drawers. My hair is wild, my face is red, and I am completely furious. Incensed. Enraged. Why would a grown woman shred her own living room? Especially a grown woman who has not yet met her lifetime goal of teaching her children to pick up after her? Why you ask? Why?

I'm looking for a tape measure.

I estimate that in my thirty-year knitting career, I have prob-ably bought/been given/acquired at least two tape measures per year. Some years, I manage to procure three or four. I purchase a tape measure every time I think of it in a sewing shop. Then I buy them whenever I can't find one. I have never, ever thrown one away, and I don't pack them off as gifts. This means that I probably own about eighty tape measures. So, I beg of you, just where the hell *are* they?

The house should be filthy with them. We should be trip-ping over them. It should be that every single time you turn around, there is another stinking tape measure. Joe should be forever asking me to manage the tape measure problem. We should be having long conversations that start with statements like, "Holy cow, Steph, do you really need all these tape meas-ures? Look at this place, for the love of wool—there's one in the bathroom and two on the landing. Get a grip." Think about it: At least eighty tape measures in this tiny house—that's about eleven and a half per room. I should have whole boxes of tape measures wrapped tenderly in colored tissue paper with little shrines above them. When people come into my home, they should start to think that I have a real but unhealthy obsession with knowing the size of things.

Instead, I have been looking for one skinny little traitorous tape measure for almost an hour and I'm starting to think that it's a plot.

That's it. It's a conspiracy. There's a club of hostile knitters who sneak into my home and take knitting notions. No—knitters wouldn't be that cruel. Would they?

I hate even to contemplate accusing my brothers and sisters in wool, but since the crime is not limited to tape measures but also includes a mind-boggling number of darning needles and stitch markers and a frightening array of double-pointed needles, it is clear to me that our perpetrator, whoever he or she is, has an interest in the needle arts.

Joe wanders into the living room and surveys the damage. Wisely, he keeps his mouth pretty much shut whenever we are having a tape measure episode.

"There are eleven and a half tape measures in this room," I fume as I dump the contents of the DVD shelf on the floor, "and I am going to find one of them if it kills me." Joe watches as I open all of the cases and look inside. "Steph?" he says. I glance up from my mission. He gives me a look. We've been married long enough that I know that look. It's his "you are starting to get a little crazy with this" face. I take a deep breath. I know that he's right.

Looking in the movie cases is a little unreasonable. It is highly unlikely that anyone who lives here would have gone to the trouble to *coil* up a tape measure, then take a case from the shelf, open it, meticulously flatten the tape measure inside, and replace the case in order simply to hide a tape measure from me. As much fun as it is to watch me completely melt down every time I need to know how long my knitting is, we are talking about a family that can't be bothered to put dishes *in* the dishwasher instead of *on* it. No, no . . . a member of this family would not hide my tape measures in such a labor-intensive way.

"I bet the kids took them," Joe offers. I try to imagine what the children would need eighty tape measures for. Some strange club? An invention? An extremely precise Maypole? It seems too implausible. I imagine the kids in a darkened corner. They have candles and they are muttering. Around them are all the tape measures, stacked in little piles.

"What would they do with my tape measures?" I ask Joe.

"What do the children do with anything?" he replies. He has a point. Anyone who has kids knows that it is not at all unusual to find three spatulas and a plastic turkey baster in the Lego bin. Children sometimes have plans that are . . . abstract, to say the least.

I start upstairs to check the Lego bin. The Lego bin turns up nothing but Legos, three Barbie shoes, a butter knife, a button off a sweater I knit last year and the screwdriver that Joe looked for all last week. I do a little better in the toy box, where I find all six pairs of my scissors. Maybe they take the tape measures and cut them into tiny bits that are easy to dispose of. It's tape measure murder. It's possible that I'd notice a whole tape measure in the garbage, but who'd see it a little at time? Perhaps they take the thousands of little snipped bits out into the world and throw them away in stages? One at the mall, two at a friend's house, three in the garbage can of the lunchroom, where the bits join all the other things that children take from their parents in order to try and put the parents into an early grave or an institution. It's possible—but again, my children are untidy enough that it's impossible that there is no evidence. There would have to be a few incriminating fragments of tape measure in the bottom of the toy box to support my theory.

I retrieve the button, the butter knife, and the six pairs of scissors. I leave the screwdriver where it is. I don't see Joe looking for my tape measures.

Dejectedly, I wander back downstairs. I'm beginning to lose my zeal for this hunt, and surveying the damage I've done to the house, I realize that stopping soon is important if I'm ever going to set things to rights. One of my pattern books has a ruler printed on the edge (Maybe they know about this problem?), and I can figure out how big the sweater is from there. I'm obviously not going to find the stupid tape measure and the only creature I haven't considered as culprit is the cat . . . and that's only because all she could do is eat them, and that seems unreasonable. Doesn't it?

Thinking of the cat inspires me. The cat is forever knocking the little bits of things that she finds to play with down the heating vents. The heating vents! I go over to one and flatten myself on the floor, squinting down into the depths. I don't see any tape measures, but they are plastic and slippery, so maybe they just tumble down to a place where there's a bend in the heating duct. That spot is so far down that there's little point in taking the cover off and reaching in. Likely all I'll discover is that I need to vacuum, and I know that without getting the handful of dusty proof.

Someday, my house will fall down and become part of history, complete with piles of plastic tape measures in the heating ducts. I'm only thirty-six, and I've lost eighty tape measures, so I figure my lifetime loss will be more than a hundred fifty. (I'm assuming an increase in tape measure responsibility in my latter years.)

There are more than 50 million knitters in North America, though I have to figure that not all of them lose tape measures at such an alarming rate, still . . . Add in Europe, and you can bet that there are more than 8 billion tape measures lost in the world right now. Eight billion of them, likely in piles, lost in the bottom of homes across the world accompanied by darning needles, stitch markers, and double-pointed needles.

A thousand years from now I imagine archaeologists working to uncover the relics of the twenty-first century. I smile to myself as I think about them trying to figure out what the strange significance of knitting must have been . . . that millions upon millions of knitters sacrificed billions upon billions of notions to the mighty heating ducts.

Spring Is Sprung

$\mathcal{T}$here is a universal message to spring, no matter where in the world you are or what kind of living thing you are. Every cell containing life all the way from grass through trees to leopards and humans receives the same message. It is a voice heard internally, pressing and insistent, and it says:

Make something.

Okay, let's look at this. For some, this is an easy one. Grass makes more grass, trees flower to make fruit, leopards make more leopards, and people . . . well, the urge is fairly clear, but the interpretation varies.

Some people clean. Their interpretation of "make something" has to do with making what they already have better. I've tried this spring-cleaning thing, but I don't find it satisfying. (Big surprise.) Frankly, diluting the make-something urge with hot soapy water weakens it for me. I empty a closet and then come to my senses with a floor full of crap I haven't seen in ten years, dust bunnies roaming like cattle, a vague sense of confusion, and no energy left for putting the mess back. Spring cleaning is not for me.

I have fallen prey to the more traditional interpretation of spring's message in the past, but much as I love my three daughters, making more of them is clearly not a long-term solution. Instead, for the last eight years I've ended up channeling this spring urge into something else: knitting. Or more specifically— Startitis. Startitis is defined as an unreasonable urge to begin new knitting projects without regard for the number of projects already begun, deadlines impending, or budgets imposed.

As the weather warms, I start getting the message. *Make something.* I resist, since I already have many, many works in progress. Starting something new is out of the question. I will finish something I have on the needles. I keep knitting, but there is something unsatisfying about it. No matter how many things I finish, the urge to cast on something new is persistent. I start bargaining with myself. "After I finish this cardigan, then I will start something." No dice. "After I finish the front of the cardigan, then?" The urge is not happy. Startitis wants me to comply. She tangles my yarn, drops the pattern under the couch twice, and sends my children in to fight while I knit. She whispers about how stupid it is to knit a cardigan when the warm weather is coming. . . . Who needs a cardigan? Startitis dreams of bright cotton and says nasty things about wool. She miscounts stitches and screws up the armhole shaping. Startitis throws a temper tantrum, and she plays ugly.

I rethink my position. Maybe Startitis is right? What am I doing? A cardigan in gray wool? Was there ever a less springlike knit? The world is coming back to life, exploding with color, and here I am, knitting a stupid gray wool cardigan? What am I, dead inside?

I snap to my senses with the realization that she almost had me there. Startitis cares nothing for me. She only wants me to begin new things. I redouble my determination to finish the cardigan, and I tell Startitis that this year, I'm using common sense. I do not need to start a new project. I can delay gratification. If I give in now, I know how it will all end. I'll cast on a whole whack of new projects and work on them until the urge passes, and then I've got a whole new problem: tons more unfinished things and it's not like Startitis's cousin Finish-it-up-itis ever comes over for a visit. No, there's no way I'm getting sucked in, not this year.

I focus on the cardigan, but Startitis isn't finished with me. While the birds sing outside, and I can smell the undeniable spring smell of melting doggie-doo, Startitis realizes that I won't be bullied. I'm a mother of three; you can't get me to cast on if I don't want to. Startitis is a wily enemy, and she knows that she must appeal to my good sense, if she wants her way.

She sends the children in. They want to go to the park; I can knit on the bench while they play. No problem, I start stuffing my cardigan into the knitting bag. It suddenly seems kind of big . . . and dull. I should really take something smaller to the park, something that will fit in my pocket . . . yeah. I need another project. I begin to drift toward the stash, maybe a hat? No, not a hat, how about that twin set, in cotton? Oh yeah, the twin set, I'm already pulling out the pattern. What cotton to use? I'm into the stash . . . there's that pale yellow cotton with the slubs, can't use that, a pale cotton for dirty park knitting? Not smart . . . how about the red that a friend bought in Italy? Naw, there's not enough . . . Wait! I could make that little shell out of the Italian cotton, and I'll stop at the yarn shop on the way to the park and get cotton for the twin set. Maybe a blue . . . like a robin's egg, that will be just the perfect spring knitting.

As I'm reaching for my credit card, I snap out of my reverie, seconds away from falling into the trap. Startled by my near-brush with perdition, I shove the cardigan into the bag and leave. My being away from home thwarts Startitis for several hours.

When I get home, Startitis has my brother phone and ask me what I'm making my mother for her birthday. Now, this is just underhanded. Have I ever missed my mother's birthday? Does Startitis think that she can trick me with this? Still, I don't realize that this is another of her attempts until I've got the Italian cotton and my hand is on the pattern shelf. As I replace the book I remind myself to stay alert. The urge is not happy about me being onto her. I look at the rest of the stuff on the shelves. There are at least five unfinished projects, from just this time last year. I know she wants me to *make something* but it's terribly misguided. Sure, I want to take part in the planet's rebirth and we all know how this will end if I go the spring-cleaning route, but it's important for me to realize that Startitis doesn't really *make* anything for me; she just gets me into knitting trouble with an unfinished project in every drawer. *But what's wrong with giving in? Why not just cast on the cotton, start another sweater . . . This is supposed to be fun, right? Crowded house be damned. Forget finishing projects—let the house be completely overrun with me and my stuff, needles and yarn everywhere. Who needs the satisfaction of finishing anything, ever!*

I sigh, then I go purposefully downstairs and pick up the cardigan. It's a nice project, and no matter what Startitis says, winter will come again, and I will want this done. I wrap the wool around my fingers and feel the soft warmth of it. I'm thinking about how much I'm going to like finishing this. Evenings are still cold in the spring.

My husband has channeled his *Make something* into finding the summer clothes and has gotten the Birkenstock sandals out. I love my Birks. I really do. It's still too cold to wear them though. I could wear them with socks . . . yeah, that's it. I don't have any really nice bright socks though. . . .

How to Succeed at Knitting
(Without Really Trying)

It's happened again. I have become cocky and proud and my knitting is suffering for it. The world is spinning crazily around me, and I'm looking at my knitting completely staggered. To stay on track for my deadline, I need to finish this slipper today. As I gleefully sail through the last row, I realize that I don't have the right number of stitches left over. This means that I've got the whole slipper crooked, and given that my mother's feet don't point inward at a forty-five-degree angle, I'm going to have to rip it back and start again. Once again, I'm furious with myself for not taking more care.

That is the knitting theme this year—rookie mistakes that shouldn't be happening to somebody who has been knitting as long as I have. These are the sorts of mistakes that you make when you're learning to knit; experienced knitters laugh about them over coffee. I've apparently decided that I am above natural knitting law. And I'm paying for it.

I've finally decided that the simple rules that every knitter needs to respect can't be outgrown. Since I can't be the only one who, over time, comes to expect experience to outweigh common sense, I've come up with a list of humbling reminders.

1. Swatching is not stupid. I cannot intuitively tell the gauge, behavior, or washability of every yarn in the world simply by holding it in my hand. Experience does not excuse me from knitting a swatch. This is obvious since I have in recent months knit a sweater that grew to seven times its original length when it hit water and a pair of socks that had ribbing so tight that they threatened mid-calf amputation.

2. It is not dumb to circle, highlight, or otherwise indicate the instructions for the size you are knitting on your pattern. I remembered this while frantically trying to think of a family member with an enormous hunchback who could wear a sweater with a size small front, and a size large back. While reknitting the front I realized that I'm disappointed that I don't know anyone misshapen enough. How weird is that?

3. Double-checking what chart symbols mean is not for losers. Just because if I ran the world, a light blue square on a chart would correspond to using light blue yarn, this does not mean that this is what the light blue square actually means.

    Sure, a horizontal line should be a purl stitch, and it's logical that no symbol means no stitch. But it ain't necessarily so, as the song says.

Shocking as it may seem, knitting designers do not have a psychic uplink with me and do not always design things the way that would be best for me personally. (On the upside of this one, while I didn't get a sweater that looked anything like the designer's, I believe I invented a new stitch pattern in an appallingly hideous colorway.)

4. It is not a waste of time to read ahead in the pattern, I do not always know what is coming. A classic example: Carefully and deliberately working the armhole decreases according to the instructions, while ever so artfully incorporating the cable pattern into my work all the way to the top, then checking the pattern for my next step and reading "at the same time" followed by the decrease directions for the neck shaping that I should have begun six inches ago.

5. Most important, I do not always know a better way to do it. Enough said. I am surrounded by an assortment of freakish knitted objects. Sweaters for which I changed the neckline to something "better" so now the neck won't go over my head. A vest for which I thought that casting off the stitches and then picking them up again for the neck was a stupid waste of time, only to learn in a horribly graphic demonstration that this alleged time-waster prevents the neckline from stretching out so much that you can step into it. Socks with drunken cables because I was overconfident about memorizing a pattern. Two left mittens. Hats for pinheads. Socks that would only fit horses.

I accept it. I will remember the rules. I will acknowledge that these are the simple mantras I must chant to myself if I want my knitting to look like the pattern. I will knit the words "Pride goeth before a fall" into a scarf of the scratchiest wool and wear it against my bare neck for a month to humble myself.

If anybody knows when the circus is passing through town, please let them know that I have a few things for them.

Yarn Requirements

To Daring Designer,
AbFabFibers, Inc.

Dear Designer,

I know how busy you are. Why just yesterday, I was admiring your new pattern for your thigh-high argyle stockings with the coordinating felted garter belt. (You are such an intriguing woman.) I won't take up much of your time, but did want to take just a moment to ask a question about some of the specifics on your sock pattern.

Why don't you and I try to agree on some basic principles? I'm not talking the big ones, like politics or world peace . . . All I want sorted out is the exact yardage on your wonderful knitting patterns. (That's a lie. I would also really like a word with the screwdriver people, I mean get real—how many kinds of screwdrivers does the world really need? Is it not possible that we could get our crap together and agree on one kind of screw? It isn't enough that I have to go looking for my screwdriver, but to need to find the small Phillips type screwdriver? It's really unnecessary.) *I know that the element of surprise is a valid part of your pattern writing, and that you don't like me to think too much for myself, but I do wonder if telling me how much yarn you used would be over the line.*

Your pattern says that I need one four-ounce skein of the lighter color and an equal amount of the dark. Your pattern even tells me that each skein of your AbFab sock yarn has about 350 yards. I appreciate your efforts (however short they may fall) to supply me with (limited) information.

My problem, my dear designer, is that I have a partial ball of your incredible sock yarn in the darker color, and I am wondering if it will be enough for the three stinking rounds that it is used for on your (as previously mentioned) wonderful pattern.

I know that this will seem odd and shocking to you, your position in the yarn world being what it is, but just try to imagine this for a moment. What if I don't want to buy a full boatload of your yarn every single time I knit one of your patterns? Naturally, since there can be no other yarn like your yarn, I wouldn't dream of trying to use another company's yarn. You should know better than anyone else that knitters never substitute yarns (right?). But is there a rule against using leftovers?

The light-colored yarn is used for the leg and foot of the sock, so I can accept that I would need a brand spanking new 350-yard skein. My question is for the darker yarn. Since it is only used for those three masterful rounds at the top of the sock, is it true that I need a full 350-yard skein, as your pattern requirements state? Or have you figured out a way to knit a black hole into the top of that sock? I wouldn't doubt it, your skills being what they are.

I know that doing this your way means that more people pur-chase more yarn, rather than using up leftovers or spinning their own, and that selling more yarn is in your best interests. I even appreciate that you need to sell me more yarn to support yourself so that you can continue your important design work. (Your Fair Isle toilet seat cover work is groundbreaking by the way—good for you, for not listening to those silly "market surveys.") But would it be completely unreasonable for me to ask whether, perhaps, I only need maybe ten yards of the darker color for the sock?

Your lady of the ~~limited~~ realistic budget,
Stephanie

P.S. Letters are a two-way street, and it wouldn't kill you to write back once in a while.

"IT"

Once again, it's Christmastime. How I can be completely blindsided by a holiday that happens on the same day each year is absolutely beyond me. You'd swear that they only announce the date for Christmas in November and I have maybe three weeks to cope with the news. Once again I am nowhere near ready, and once again my family has turned its back on me.

I can't really blame the poor embattled souls; they have been down this road with me before and they know how it ends. I know how it ends too. "IT" is the bane of our holidays. Every year I swear that "IT" will never happen again, that I will learn from my experience. It seems I can't be taught.

Even as I write, I don't believe that "IT" will happen to me this year. This year will be different. This year I can do it.

Here's how "IT" begins. Sometime in the fall, when the weather gets crisp and wearing wool starts to make sense again, I realize that Christmas is coming and I'd better get started on the holiday knitting. (Mind you, if everyone pitched in and did something about global warming I might get more of a heads-up, but never mind.) Usually I voice this happy concern as I begin taking apart the stash, leaving stacks of patterns and yarn around the house, and further neglecting housework and my real job. Every year I am convinced that this time, I have started early enough to avoid "IT." I plan all kinds of things. Little sweaters for babies I know, hats for quick gifts, socks to keep darling feet warm and afghans for new homes. (That's right—afghans. Hope springs eternal.)

Thus we enter Phase 1. Phase 1 is a happy time. I am planning; I love my wool and patterns; I am full of good ideas; I bask in the pleasure of expressing my love through wool. Christmas is far enough away. Phase 1 is joy.

Phase 2 involves detailed planning and casting on. During Phase 2, I start making lists. What exactly do I plan on knitting before Christmas? Here is this year's list:

- Four pairs of felted clogs (brother, sister-in-law, aunt, and uncle)
- One afghan (brother with new house)
- One throw (sister with new house)
- Three hoodie sweaters (daughters)
- One shawl (mother-in-law)
- Two sets of hats and mittens (nieces)
- Three sweaters (nephew, goddaughter, friend's baby)
- Hat and scarf (daughter's tutor)
- Five washcloths (daughters' teachers)
- Two pairs of socks (mate, best friend)

- Elegant copper and gold wrap (myself, to go with my little black dress)

This last item marks the depths of my delusion. Not only does it rest on the illusion that I will be invited somewhere where this is appropriate attire, but it assumes that I will get through the mountain of knitting I've planned with enough time not just to knit the wrap but to go out wearing it.

Then I go through the stash and to the yarn store and cast on all of these projects (usually in one day), place them strategically around the house so that I have the right kind of knitting in each room, and happily begin knitting. Phase 2 is when my family starts laughing and shaking their heads. Phase 2 is when I tell them that this year will be different.

Phase 3 is when it starts to get ugly. Phase 3 is when I look at the projects scattered around the house and start to feel the first pangs of concern. It dawns on me that this may be a fairly large (read "impossible") enterprise. This is the phase in which my family stops laughing and starts the nervous giggling as it slowly dawns on them that "IT" is going to happen again. I handle Phase 3 by rationalizing and planning. Some common rationalizations are "Well, I know it looks like a lot, but the afghan is on big needles" or "I've never knit felted clogs, but they can't take more than an hour a pair." The planning is more vague. I'll knit on the bus; my mate will do the laundry to free up time; I'll knit for thirty minutes on each thing, and it will all go so quickly. I can do it. It will be fine. I'm a fast knitter and this is reasonable. . . . Right?

Phase 4 is when the support of my family goes out the window. Phase 4 is when it finally occurs to me that I might have a knitting crisis. Being the hopeful type, I'm still fairly positive. I know I have a problem, but I believe that with a serious commitment I can get out of it. It is in this phase that my family starts to express concern for my physical health and mental well-being. They begin to talk about how "IT" was last year. Phase 4 strategies include the following:

1. Carefully assess project status and estimate how many hours of knitting remain. Divide this number by the number of days until Christmas. (When figuring the number of knitting days available to you, allow every day between now and Christmas, even though you know that you will have to spend some days doing other things. Denial is a powerful Phase 4 tool.) This gives you the KHPD (Knitting Hours Per Day) that you must knit to meet your Christmas goal. (Tip: Make sure that you underestimate the number of hours it will take you to knit your items; you don't want to scare yourself.)

2. Neglect housework. This can increase knitting time substantially, but you must remember to deduct one day from your total number of days until Christmas to clean up for the guests.

3. Deduct sleeping time. Minor sleep deprivation is okay here. People with new babies miss all kinds of sleep. It won't kill you. I find that I can convert one hour of sleep to knitting time every night without any real consequences.

4. Make sure your family knows that you are going to be knitting full time. Make known the gravity of the situation. My personal technique for this consists of showing everyone the list repeatedly and explaining in a maniacal tone of voice that I am going to need some extra help and consideration. Ignore their pleas for sanity. If they beg you to stop and ask you please, for the love of God, not to let "IT" happen this year, ask them if they are trying to ruin Christmas.

Some holiday knitters never make it to Phase 5. Phase 5 is the final stage before "IT" overwhelms a knitter. In Phase 4, there is the lurking knowledge that this may not be possible, but during Phase 5 this concern becomes outright terror. Phase 5 is the first time that you actually think "Oh-oh, I might not make it."

What are some Phase 5 symptoms?

1. You have decided, calmly and reasonably, that it makes total sense to deduct another three hours of sleep per day to increase your knitting time.

2. You have decided that having all your meals delivered is a smart move.

3. You have canceled your attendance at the Christmas party because it will reduce knitting time. Not because you can't knit at the party, but because you can't justify losing the knitting time to take a shower and put on a dress.

4. You aren't entirely sure where your children are, and you may be losing touch with caring about it.

5. You start calculating how many stitches per minute you need to knit if you are going to make it.

The most profound symptom of Phase 5 is project modification. Scarf and hat sets become just scarves, or just hats, whatever I have done. Sweaters become vests, afghans become throws—you get the picture. Knitters in Phase 5 do not give up completely; they just work out what needs to be knit smaller or out of chunky yarn on bigger needles.

Each year during Phase 5 my family makes their last appeal. They beg me not to lose touch. They tell me that there is more to life than knitting and that people would rather I was well rested and happy than making them socks. They tell me that the sooner I give up, the sooner I can enjoy some of the holiday. They tell me that I am on the brink of "IT." My husband rubs my back and tells me that it really isn't as important as I think to finish all this knitting.

I ignore their lies. They are not on my side; I can tell.

And then I enter "IT."

"IT" is a far and perilous place known only to the most determined and obsessive knitters. I don't know for sure how many knitters have experienced "IT," but no matter how many of us there are, "IT" still feels like a dark and lonely place. The difference between "IT" and regular holiday deadlines is like the difference between a stress headache and having your head squeezed in a drill press.

"IT" questions go like this:

1. How many hours will it be before people open their gifts? ("IT" usually takes place only in the three days before Christmas; anything before that gives you enough time to save yourself and is therefore still Phase 5.)

2. How many things are left unknit? ("IT" always has multiple items. If you are just trying to finish one gift . . . well, good for you.)

3. Does your KHPD (Knitting Hours Per Day) required to finish in time for Christmas now exceed twenty-four?

If you are truly experiencing "IT," the following will also be true:

1. Despite having calculated your KHPD, and realizing that you cannot possibly finish in time, you are still knitting instead of sleeping.

2. You have actually not slept since you entered "IT," and depending on your type, you have also given up eating, or you have only eaten chocolate and leftover pizza crusts for the last several days.

3. The children will be up in forty-five minutes to see what Santa brought them and you are sitting wild-eyed in the

darkened house frantically knitting the hats you want to put in their stockings.

4. You are prioritizing the knitting according to when you will see the recipient. For example: You don't see your aunt until the evening of the twenty-fifth, but you see your mother in the afternoon. Therefore, since it is only the twenty-fourth you are working on your husband's socks because you will see him first thing on Christmas morning. You have actually come to believe that this means that you have *lots of time* until you need your aunt's present.

5. You are planning to sew your nephew's sweater together in the basement while everyone else opens gifts. You are pretty sure that as long as they all go first you can make it.

6. Finally, you have vowed that next year you will start sooner, do less, and be more realistic about your knitting goals. You have vowed that you will not ruin Christmas by dedicating your life to the pursuit of woolen gifts for everyone. You admit that it may be possible to buy your aunt's dog a gift next year instead of knitting it a sweater. Furthermore, you have admitted that while this plan looked like fun when you started, you are not having much fun now. You admit that your refusal to go skating with the children, because tying skates up cuts into knitting time, may be affecting their happiness as well. You have also agreed with your spouse that it is reasonable to expect that you would have time for "marital

relations" at least once during the month of December, and you know that this means you will have to knit less. You have also admitted that you cannot warp the time-space continuum, despite the persistent belief and occasional proof that it is possible.

In short you have promised that next year you will not do "IT." Never again.

But you will, and I will be here for you. I promise.

Sour Grapes

Although I am, in general, a loving and tolerant yarn person, I cannot abide crochet. I know that this may shock and upset those of you who have fallen under its hooked spell, but crochet gives me hives. (I have not ever actually gotten hives while crocheting, but I swear that I could feel them starting.) While I have many reasons for hating crochet, I have to be honest: A big part of my disdain may have something to do with my abject failure to crochet properly. Not one piece I've crocheted has been even remotely passable. Being pro-yarn, I will try just about anything in the wool family of activities, but each and every one of my forays into crochet has ended badly. There are doilies of which we shall not speak, and nightmarish episodes in which I tried to make something with a ruffle called an antimacassar. That was especially bad, possibly because I have no idea what a "macassar" is, much less why I should be against it.

The important point here is that knitting and crochet are not the same. Just because they are both about yarn and making stuff out of it, they don't share the same skill set. Despite the general public's inability to tell them apart (Have you noticed that knitters on TV are often producing crocheted objects?), they are as different as chickens and vertical blinds.

Not everyone feels the way that I do. There are turncoats. Double agents. Knitters who put crochet edgings on things, or crocheters who sometimes knit socks. There are even those who freely move between the camps, knitting, crocheting, and occasionally dallying with quilts or plastic canvas. I am not a double agent. I believe that knitting is superior to crochet. I pledge allegiance to the knitted swatch, and nothing you can say about crochet will convince me to try again. I am now anti-antimacassar (Up with "macassars"!). I still keep a crochet hook around, but I only use it to pick up the occasional dropped stitch. I always try to pick up the stitch without the crochet hook first, and I feel a little bit dirty if I have to give up and use it.

It's time that someone told the truth about crochet and what it can lead to. Who better to set the record straight than a completely biased knitter who has never had a single positive crochet experience? Let's examine a few facts about crochet and see if we can set the record straight.

Crochet devotees claim that it is faster than knitting. Okay. You have me here. Crocheting does make better time, if we are simply assessing square footage per hour. I know that there are millions of knitters out there who are halfway through an afghan that is sucking the very life out of them. If you are one of them, you just sat up straight in your knitting chair and said, "Really?" and are now suddenly considering a whole lifestyle change—but wait! Think of the ethics of it. Crochet may be faster, but that's because crocheters long ago devised underhanded "double" and "triple" crochet. I beg you knitters to search for your inner maturity. Speed appeals to the immature crafter who cannot delay gratification. Knitting's simplicity, its reliance on the Zen yin and yang of knit and purl, is its nobility and no matter how incredibly stupidly slow it seems at times, it's worth it. Knitting evokes the true artist's commitment. You need to really hunker down with knitting and put in some serious time before you see results. Cabling and Fair Isle, both time takers, rank higher than straight stockinette. In this sense, "double knitting" may be knitting's highest achievement, taking twice the work and producing a double layer of knitted fabric. Knitting gives away nothing for free. Clearly, knitting is for crafters who have attention spans, and can plan ahead. Besides, if we wanted fast, we could just buy the danged socks.

In my opinion (which I have admitted isn't even slightly fair), high-speed crochet can lead directly to poor project choices. How carefully are you going to consider your final product if it only takes three hours to make a king-sized bedspread? A knitter will be spending 154 hours to cover the same area. You're not going to take on that sort of project on a whim, not with that sort of time commitment, and you're going to think through your color choices. Few and far between are the knitters who are willing to spend thirty-four hours making a Southern belle toilet paper cover, but you see it in crochet all the time. The speed of crochet leads to projects that can be executed so quickly that they don't get due consideration. With knitting, you cast on and knit for a while; you're only a few rows in before you realize that you must have been having a stroke when you put those colors together. Two rows you can walk away from. Crochet is so fast that there is no time to think it through. After a couple of hours you've got half a slipcover for the couch. Who's going to do away with that? I'm telling you, the quickness of this craft leads to reckless stitching. If you don't believe me, I can mail you a crochet pattern for a Santa Claus toilet seat cover. It would take a knitter weeks to knit it, plenty of time to come to your senses. But with crochet? Three glasses of wine, one bad idea, and whammo; two hours later you've created a festive Father Christmas commode cover and a legacy. Speed kills.

Another bad thing about crochet: It uses three times more yarn than knitting to cover the same area. *Three times.* Can you afford that? Is this an economical and respectful use of the sheep? I believe that this viciously unnecessary cost leads crocheters to live cruel lives; they are forced to have smaller stashes of lesser quality or to work long hours of overtime to support painful yarn habits that are three times bigger than they have to be. You know what average knitters have to go through just to tuck away enough wool to be sure that they don't run out in their golden years—storing away bits and balls of yarn for forty or even fifty years, still driven to purchase more at every opportunity, still wondering if they'll have enough. Now imagine trying to come up with three times that amount of stash. Will your children have enough food? What about their educations? Where will your spouse live when his or her side of the home is filled with your huge stash? Switch to knitting and save yourself. Or if that doesn't move you, switch to knitting and your stash will go three times as far. Frankly, I'm concerned about the possibility that some sort of yarn cartel is responsible for hooking (pun intended) young crocheters into these big yarn habits.

There are other drawbacks. Crochet burns 80 calories per hour, knitting uses 85. Over twenty years, assuming that you will knit or crochet one hour a day, that means that knitting burns 36,500 more calories. That's a lot of chocolate. Who needs more incentive than that? Crochet uses one hook. Knitting requires two needles, sometimes more. Impress your friends, frighten your family, think of the glory of multiple tools!

If that still doesn't do it, think of the danger. Crochet never hurt anyone, but knitting? Knitting is full of tales of risk and harm. Knitters even occasionally suffer not just devastating pokes, but shallow impalings. It's even conceivable that you could put an eye out. Crochet, with its rounded gentle hooks is playing it safe. Which is more exciting, a James Bond knitting adventure or Winnie the Pooh play-nice crochet?

It's all about the combination of elements. The deadly mix of easy, fun, fast, and yarn-consuming is not where you want to go. This setup can lead to only one end: a desperate crafter, moving at the speed of sound on a wicked yarn high, making poor project choices he or she can ill afford. Before you know it, the evil lure of crochet with its quirky granny squares and fetching shell edgings has ensnared you. You find yourself making a ripple pattern freezer cozy out of the 100 percent petroleum knitting product you had left over from the toilet cover and you think you're having fun.

Trust me, you're not.

Socks for Sinead

My friend Sinead claims to be allergic to wool. This assertion has caused a few problems in our relationship. Admittedly, the problems are mostly mine, since I am simply incapable of believing her. I can't fathom it. She's allergic to *all* wool? She's Irish, for crying out loud—is that even possible? All those centuries of fine woolens being produced, worn, and revered by millions and millions and millions of Irish, and she says she's allergic?

It's not possible I tell you. I don't believe it. I had some heated debates about this with Sinead, and I've got to tell you that she didn't make a good case for her supposed "allergy." She said wool made her itch. "That's not an allergy," I asserted firmly. "Some wool is scratchy. Some wool makes *me* itch. You can't blacken an entire fiber group because someone gave you bad wool. What about merino? Have you tried merino?" I glared at her across the table. Allergic to wool, my arse. I'm a loving person, but I wouldn't have my beloved slandered right in front of me without putting up a fight.

Sinead reiterated gravely, "All wool, Steph. *All* wool makes me itch. I can't wear wool. I'm allergic. Knit me something with cotton or acrylic."

Baloney. Instead of deciding to call my dear friend a rotten stinking liar over tea, instead of telling her that for me to take her "allergy" seriously I needed to see swelling and hives and maybe a little anaphylactic wheezing, instead of speaking to her of her Celtic woolen heritage and her honor—instead I sipped my tea and accepted the challenge. I would get wool on Sinead, and she would see the goodness of it, and I would be right—not that being right was the point, though I really love to be right.

What's not to love about wool?

For starters, think of one incredible fact. The world has come a long way, and astonishing and intriguing machines arrive every day, but there is still not a machine on this earth that will shear a sheep. Every ball of wool starts with some man or woman somewhere in the world, a complete stranger to you, holding fast to a pissed-off sheep while cutting its fleece free. Every single ball. Just imagine it. Every ball of wool you and I have ever knit, all the balls of wool in the world in every country in the whole history of the world thus far, came from the sweat and grit of a person wrestling a hot, dirty, furious sheep.

Second, wool is light, warm when it is wet, and miraculously, incredibly real. Acrylic yarn is to wool as Twinkies are to wholegrain bread. It's fun every now and then, but you can't live on it. Itchy? Isn't a little itch (except that there are nonitchy wools out there) worth it for the benefits of wool? What Sinead needed to learn was that there was wool, and then, there was *wool*.

To establish Sinead's actual baseline itch level, I knit a hat. I dug into the stash and came up with a plain, good wool. I knit it in a pattern that I knew she would love and want to wear. I knit it in a color that went with her coat, and I gave it to her on a very cold day (to make it as tempting as possible). Sinead was flattered. She was a little perplexed by this gift of a wool hat, what with it being so soon after the "allergy" conversation but my friends are used to being confused, and she did put the hat on. This reinforced my theory that she wasn't actually allergic—do you see people with peanut allergies giving peanuts a whirl every now and again just to see how it goes?

She wore the hat for a while, but developed a weird sort of salute as she rubbed the itch on her forehead every few minutes. Okay. So she's a little sensitive. I wasn't disappointed, since the purpose of the hat was really only to see if she knew what she was talking about and if she was telling the truth.

Nobody said this would be easy. I went back to the yarn shop and began to hunt around for the softest wool I could find. I spent a good deal of time in the shop, rubbing skeins of yarn against the tender skin of my forearm and holding them briefly against my neck. I found a merino that made the "basic" wool seem as harsh as a girl's first date, and I bought it with confidence. I did briefly discuss my mission with the shop owner (who wondered why I would be rubbing yarn on the sensitive skin of my lower back). For the record, she agreed that Sinead merely needed education. Back home I knit the merino into a lacy scarf (loose stitches are bound to be softer) and packed it off to my victim—er, friend. I was feeling optimistic. It took a long time to choose that yarn. It was Italian, expensive, and quite luscious. That wool was to regular wool as the ceiling of Michelangelo's Sistine Chapel is to the paint job in my bathroom. Sinead was going to love it—how could she not? It's a crepe merino.

I awaited word.

The next time I saw Sinead, I noticed that she was wearing the scarf rather guiltily on the outside of her coat, where it lay quite elegantly but did not touch her skin. It was at this point that I started to wonder if she were running a scam. A huge cosmic "getting knitted stuff" scam, since it had occurred to me that the more things she found itchy the more things I was going to be compelled to knit for her. I started thinking (and possibly saying out loud) things like "never say die" and "try, try again." Sinead looked worried as I stomped off looking especially driven, though I can't imagine why. This was all for her own good.

I got to thinking about socks. Handknit socks are such a luxury that I can't think of Sinead or anyone else turning them down just to make a point (which I had increasingly come to believe was true in this case).

Finding the softest sock yarn in the history of the world is not a game for the impatient, and it took (understandably) quite some time. I looked for Sinead's sock yarn all through the summer, scouring Toronto's yarn shops—going further afield, to Kingston, Ottawa, Hull, Montreal. I expanded the scope of my search as my family traveled through Canada's eastern provinces, New Brunswick, Prince Edward Island, Newfoundland. But it was in Nova Scotia that I hit pay dirt. The sock yarn I found there was so lovely that if you had told me that angels flew it down from heaven twice a week to try and make up for poison ivy, I would consider that a reasonable explanation. It is so beautiful and soft that I would not hesitate (except for the nagging concern that people would think I was a raving lunatic) to knit it into underpants. As I began knitting the socks for Sinead I thought to myself, *this yarn wouldn't itch if it was diapers on a four-day-old baby.*

When I smugly gave Sinead her socks, I knew in my heart that this time I'd got her. Not only were the socks soft, but they had been rated nonitchy by each and every test subject who had tried them on.

"Not one negative review," I told Sinead cheerfully. Now she'd know about wool. She was going to thank me for this. This was really a poignant moment for me, sitting on the floor shoving the socks onto her feet (Sinead had inexplicably demonstrated some resistance).

"Maybe I could try them later?" Sinead asked, with her toes curling up. "I'm really running a little late and I didn't know you were coming with the socks so I . . ." Her voice trailed off. I glanced at her as I whipped her old left sock off and wondered why she kept looking at the door. Never mind, I thought, working the sock on over her heel. Besides being the softest socks in the world, these were among the most beautiful, rainbows of muted colors. Wool at its best—it brought tears to my eyes.

I would like it noted that up to that point, I didn't really have a plan. I was just an ordinary obsessive knitter trying to spread the gift of the sheep throughout the world, that all people might know the same joy that I had found in woolen goods. I only wanted to bring happiness and knitted love to Sinead's life and straighten out her little "allergy" idea. That's all I was after—right up until the exact moment, not more than ten seconds after I had those socks on her legs, long before the sock molecules could possibly have made their way to her immune system . . . when Sinead reached down and quietly scratched her sock-clad leg.

Seldom in my life have I had such a moment of sparkling clarity. As I watched her discreet efforts to rip the not-at-all itchy socks off her body, it hit me. I finally understood. After all of those tries and all of that time and all of that knitting, I finally got the allergy thing.

Sinead *believed* that she was allergic to wool and the mind was a powerful force. Clearly (since we all know that a wool allergy is too ridiculous a concept to entertain), Sinead had a psychosomatic illness. Since my past attempts to convince people to seek professional help because they did not feel the way that I do about wool have rarely succeeded, I began to think about . . . let's be honest, here . . . a little white lie.

Now, as a general rule, I'm a very honest person. I don't lie as a matter of course, and I certainly don't take lightly the idea of leading a friend into a web of deceit.

But desperate times call for desperate measures. If Sinead had a bias against wool, whether she knew it or not, she wasn't giving the wool a fair shake. There was no freaking way those socks could be itchy. Sinead was pretty quick to pass judgment on the scarf too, now that I thought about it. Her subconscious (probably scarred by some horrible cheap wool in her youth) was projecting itchiness where there was none. Therefore, anything Sinead believed to be wool was going to itch. Deceiving her was perfectly ethical; it was like having a double blind or a placebo in a real experiment.

I started to think of a plan. Naturally, I didn't tell Sinead about it. I didn't tell her of my plan to trick her. I simply said, "Okay, Sinead, I give up."

I started to do my research. I learned about micron fiber measurement and blood count and sheep breeds. I learned that Corriedale is an average fleece and that Cotswald is only good for rugs or outerwear. I constructed wild fiber nightmares of the infant Sinead swaddled in a coarse Cotswald blanket. I imagined the exact nature, color, and breed of the sheep that must have done this to her. Mostly, however, I was busy enjoying my new hobby, which consisted of asking every knitter and spinner I met what the softest fleece in the world was. Some of them answered in long dreamy soliloquies. Some of them begged off without an answer. Some of them got annoyed because I asked them twice. But when they heard about poor wool-deprived Sinead, they all promised to keep an eye out. I kept an eye out too. While the search was sometimes wearing, it comforted me to think of all of the knitters out there in the world looking for the magic fleece that would convert Sinead.

One fine day, I met up with an especially sympathetic spinning friend who had with her a largish garbage bag. In this bag, she told me, her voice low and trembling, was a fleece.

"A Merino-Targhee cross." At the words, she got a tic over her eye and looked wildly out the coffeeshop windows. "Did you see someone there?" she whispered urgently. "I got the last one for you," she said, giggling a little.

"Thanks," I muttered comfortingly. I was always glad to get a fleece.

"You don't understand," she said, clearly appalled at my cavalier attitude. Lowering her voice and speaking with hushed reverence, she said, "It's the softest fleece in the world. You don't know what it cost, you don't know who else wanted it. You don't understand." She puffed up with pride. "I got it for Sinead." She giggled again.

I took the bag and left. I did feel a little bad for what Sinead's illness had cost my fellow knitters and spinners, but victory has its price.

Once home, I realized what I had. Inside the bag was a little tag with the names of the shepherdess, the contributing sheep, and its parents. Fleece sheep (not meat sheep) are bred for fleece quality the way that racehorses are bred for speed. This sheep's parents were the Secretariat and Seabiscuit of the sheep world. This fleece was not just a fleece; it was a legend. It looked and felt like cobwebs or dandelion fluff or cotton balls. It was going to be perfect.

Fast forward several weeks, during which I washed the fleece by tiny immaculate handfuls in the kitchen sink, spread it in the sunshine to dry, carded it by hand with my finest cards (no drumcarder for this prize) and began to spin it into fine, fine yarn. As I worked I imagined Sinead's face when she put on the socks I would knit with this yarn. In the fantasy, joy and relief spread across her face as she tells me that these socks are like a symphony. A masterwork. As I began to knit them, my mind's eye could see her expression melt as the socks slid up over her feet and ankles. She wonders at the beauty of them, the simple perfection of them. The short-row heel, the seamless grafted toe, the ribbing that clings so softly to her leg . . . She begs me for more. She believes, as she marvels at the simple ribbed genius on her leg, that not only does she now love wool (and completely sees my point and concedes that I was right all along), but she also thinks the socks make her legs look really slender. In some of my daydreams, Sinead cries tears of happiness.

One sparkling crisp fall day, I finished the socks. I phoned Sinead and tried to act casual. "Coffee?" I said casually. "Wool?" she asked anxiously. I laughed what I hoped sounded like a little light laugh. "No, no . . . I told you, I gave up." Sinead laughed too, with what sounded more like relief than happiness, and agreed to meet me.

When we met for coffee that day I tried not to think too much about what was going to happen. I tried not to seem too invested. Casually, I slid the bag with the socks in it across the table, as though they meant nothing to me. Sinead looked warily at the bag and pulled her purse a little closer to her, as though she was thinking about making a break for it.

"What's this?" she said, tentatively extending her hand toward the bag, the way a trained expert approaches a bomb.

That's when I said it. That's when I put it all on the line. The perfect small moment that I'd been waiting for hung in the air between us. It was now or never, the work and search and commitment of a whole team of knitters and spinners—it all came down to now. Trembling a little, I said the two words: "Cotton socks."

Sinead looked around her for the hidden camera. "Really?"

"Yes" (two lies). "I understand about the wool" (three lies) "and I wanted you to know I'm sorry about all the woollies" (four lies).

Sinead reached into the bag and pulled out those soft, perfect socks—socks that, now they were done, were only (if at all possible) softer than the fleece that I had started with. I had spun them with the utmost care. Not too much twist to make them feel hard, three plies to make the yarn seem rounder and soft. They were like the pillows of angels, the clouds of a summer sky, the soft new skin of a baby's tummy.

She took them out of the bag and ran her hands over them, then slid a hand inside. My heart was pounding, but I sipped my coffee and looked nonchalantly at the pastries.

"Steph," she finally said, "these are beautiful. Thank you."

"You're welcome," I replied, and then we ate Danishes and chatted about things that didn't matter.

A full week, I waited. Seven whole days, when I resisted the growing urge to drop by Sinead's house and catch her wearing the socks. Seven days that I waited for the phone to ring and to hear Sinead's grateful voice on the other end, calling to tell me (her voice catching with emotion) that the socks have changed her life, that she loves these cotton socks above all else. Seven long days during which I practice my "*A-ha!*" speech, the speech I'd been working on for months—the one in which I tell her that the socks are wool, not cotton.

Sinead is unbelieving at first, and shocked, but then gratitude spreads through her as she realizes that I have freed her from the nightmare of a life without wool. It is delicious anticipation. I wait eagerly for my moment.

Sinead doesn't call. By the seventh day I know why she is silent. It's not because she doesn't want to call. No; it's because she can't find the words to tell me how she feels. She loves the socks so much that she is beyond words.

I decided to free her. I dropped by that afternoon to see her in the socks and was gobsmacked almost beyond all decency to see that she was not wearing the socks. Had she worn them out already? A single nauseating moment of horror swept over me: Perhaps, having accepted the cotton lie, she'd machine-washed them, and my deceit had been revealed when she pulled half-size felted booties out of the dryer. I sweated while she made coffee. I looked around (discreetly) for the evidence.

Sinead gave nothing up. If she knew about the lie, she certainly wasn't telling. I waited another horrible two minutes and then I went for broke: I asked about the socks. As casually as possible, without even making eye contact, I said it.

"How are you liking those socks?" and then I held my coffee cup and I waited.

I'd spent probably a hundred hours trying to bring the joy of wool to my beloved friend. I'd lied, and worse than that, I'd corrupted other knitters into helping me lie. I'd given up whole days of my life washing sheep crap out of a legendary fleece in my kitchen sink and had worn my fingers raw spinning it. The limp in my left leg from all the treadling still hadn't gone away. I'd spent time, money, and most of my pride—and here we were in Sinead's kitchen, and she was holding the moment I craved. I sipped my coffee; I tried to breathe slowly and evenly and this time, I looked her dead in the eye.

She looked back. Then she sighed and said, "They are *so* beautiful, Steph. But I have to tell you . . ."

The world stopped turning and my heart skipped four beats. This was my moment . . .

"They're the itchiest cotton socks I've ever had."

four

War and Pieces:
Or, You Can't Win Them All

What Her Hands Won't Do

𝒯here is treasure on the floor.

I am in my friend Lene's apartment with her and my friend Ken, and there is treasure on the floor. Now, if you are not a Knitter (and you must note the capital K, for there are people who knit and there are Knitters and the two are very different) you might think that what's on the floor is yarn, but the three of us, Ken, Lene, and I, are Knitters, and we know treasure when we see it.

Usually, when I see riches like these, I know just what to do with it: Stuff my pockets and run. If I can't be sure of a clean getaway, I speak reverently of the yarn and hope that someone will give me some. This day, though, it's different.

I don't know if I want this yarn.

It's crazy not to want it. I want all yarn, even ugly yarn, and this yarn isn't ugly. There is alpaca the color of chocolate milk, linen from Denmark, hand-dyed mohair in a shade of blue that reminds me of that particular blue of baby eyes, and much more, each skein tantalizing and special. It's all so beautiful. It's a whole life laid out in yarn.

Lene is giving it all away. Ken and I are supposed to divvy it up and take it. All of it. Despite my knitterly imperative to cavort and stuff my bags full, I can hardly touch it.

Lene is giving away her whole stash because Lene has rheumatoid arthritis. Although its vicious workings have confined her to a wheelchair, I have never considered her disabled (just nonwalking) until today.

Lene's hands won't do it anymore. They are exhausted and knotted and tired, and they won't knit.

I can't imagine giving up knitting. I simply can't. I try to imagine what I would do if I didn't knit. How would I fill those hours? How could I not be knitting? If I had to give up knitting I'd certainly have to take smoking up again—maybe heroin . . . I certainly would be ruder and wait less patiently. I think about all the time I've spent waiting in my life. I think about arriving at the doctor's office and having to bide my time; instead of being frustrated and angry, I'm grateful. I pull the sock from my purse and turn the waiting time into footwear that will warm the feet of someone I love . . . maybe Lene. She's always been my favorite person to knit socks for, since she doesn't walk in them and wear them out. The softest yarn—yarn too soft to knit socks from, really—makes perfect socks for Lene. She'll never wear through a heel. There are advantages to not walking. You get the best socks.

Lene has always appreciated the socks that I knit her. A Knitter herself, she knows how hard-won the vine lace borders on her latest pair are. She understands the sacredness of her dragon socks, because we had a long talk about the difficulties of knitting the tail that curves around her ankle. Lene is Danish, and the Danes know knitting. She learned to knit as a little girl in school where (be still my beating heart) knitting was a *subject*. She often mocked non-Danish Knitters like me and laughs at our patterns. A Danish pattern, she told me, doesn't spoon-feed the knitter. It might say "After the leg, make the heel," with no further clue as to what might be required. "Make the heel?" I asked her. "Just 'Make the heel'?" That doesn't seem like a lot to go on. As a matter of fact, it seems a little scary. Danish Knitters expect you to have more nerve. They expect you to know how to make a heel. Even if you missed that day in school, your friends know, your mother knows, your neighbor next door can teach you. My head is filled with little Danish girls turning out socks that rival my own. I know about the Danish love of candles and family, and I imagine a whole country of cozy Knitters quietly turning heels by candlelight in the long mild winter. Lene is Danish, and I wonder how she feels, thwarted by her tired hands, having to give up knitting.

Lene and I don't talk much about this, this huge scary Not Knitting. When the trouble started, it unsettled me so much that I tried to fix it. Shorter needles, bigger needles. Plastic, then metal, then soft, warm wood. I counseled her against cotton, telling her that it was too inelastic. "Switch to soft wool," I suggested. "It's easier on your hands."

Nothing worked. Knitting hurt.

I tried hard to absorb these two words. "Knitting. Hurt." That couldn't be right. Knitting couldn't be hurting her hands. Knitting soothed. Knitting was magic. Knitting took idle moments and made them worthwhile. Knitting made stupid moments smart. Knitting was whole hours spent turning dumb useless string into shawls and scarves and mittens that warmed hands and proved love. Knitting could *hurt*?

My struggle to understand was nothing compared to Lene's struggle to accept. Her body was antagonistic. Its goals weren't the same as hers. She wanted to go; it wanted to stop. She wanted to travel; it wanted to stay home. She was about speed and quickness and cleverness, but her body disagreed. It was too busy turning itself into knots to take up her causes. It took away walking and dancing and skating. It took away running and climbing trees and getting Lene out of bed in the morning. It took so much, but it left knitting. Knitting was the one thing her hands would still do. They might be knotted and tired, but they could still make stitches. The body that wouldn't skip or waltz or do stairs could still take a ball of soft yarn and two needles and take the time to make neat, even stitches in order. Mittens, scarves, and baby things came away from Lene's needles, as perfect and orderly as she dreamed. Lene took this as proof that her body was not all bad, not completely the enemy. As long as she could knit, there was still this one thing, this small proof that she was not simply a marvelous brain atop a useless carriage.

Now, suddenly, knitting hurt, and no modification of the art helped. I gave Lene better and better wool and she bought heaps of it herself, both of us somehow thinking that temptation would lead her rebel hands back to the art of wrapping wool around needles and leaving socks in their wake. But nothing worked, not one thing.

Now, months after knitting her last stitch, Lene is giving away her stash.

Ken and I are torn. We both want to make her laugh, to forget that this is the end of making things. We want to forget that this is the moment when we all admit that her arthritis has, in this matter, gotten the better of her. We fight over the wool, but neither of us wants to take it. We get two bins, mine and his, and we start to divide the yarn. Lene tells us the story of each yarn as we take it, and slowly, we start to feel better. For the moment we are soothed, lost in the tale each yarn has to tell us.

We pay attention to Lene's wishes. That blue mohair, the one the color of baby eyes, it was supposed to be a shawl for Lene's friend Michelle. I take that one. I lay it in the bin and make a mental note: Shawl for Michelle. Ken gets the discontinued Aran-weight tweed. Lene had planned an intricately cabled pullover for herself with that yarn. I watch Ken; he's making the same note-to-self, recording carefully what Lene's intentions were. The chocolate milk alpaca (a scarf for Lene's mother, Bea) goes into my bin and we laugh at the collection of bright, plain good wool in crayon colors that Ken puts in his. Lene has no idea what she was thinking for that. Sock yarn, mitten yarn, needles, and patterns, Ken and I sort them according to who likes what.

Getting this much free yarn should be a blast; I should be loving it. But it's horrible. It's a wake for Lene's knitting.

When the evening ends, Ken and I each have a big bin of Lene's wool. A whole knitting career divided into two big bins and a couple of bags. There is no evidence of Lene's life as a Knitter left in the apartment. I try hard not to feel like we are taking all hope with us. Rheumatoid arthritis is a progressive disease; Lene knows she will not knit again and I understand her urge to see the wool meet happy and productive ends. Ken and I make a couple of lame jokes on the way out the door ("We'd like to thank arthritis for making this stash enhancement possible."), but I'm pretty sure Lene cried when we left.

Months later, it's almost Michelle's birthday, and the baby blue eyes mohair is on my needles. Ken's got a hat for Lene's sister on the go. Lene's yarn might be in my stash, but it isn't my stash. I knit it for birthdays and Christmas and special events, and on the tag it always reads "from Lene." We are proxy Knitters, Ken and I; we are making up for what her hands won't do.

Freakin' Birds

$\mathcal{N}$ot too long ago, shortly after Christmas, when I was feeling generous, I was approached by a friend with a knitting crisis. I now feel confident that he chose his victim and his timing carefully. He knows me too well.

First, he knew that having been pushed to the edge of sanity by "IT" and then barely rescued by sleep, I was bound to be vulnerable and weak. Second, he knew that knitting crises are second nature to me; since I am usually plagued by disaster and upset, I might not notice this one. Third, he knew the secret words and was not afraid to use them.

"I need you to finish this. I can't knit it. It's too hard."

There they are, the magic words: "It's too hard." Ya got me. I know, I know. I'm going to get a T-shirt that says "Pride goeth before a fall," and wear it every day for a month.

Since I was still riding a high that came from blocking a lace shawl, I took the bait.

He dragged out his knitting bag, and dumped the knitting reject onto the floor. I recognized it immediately. It was the Bird Jacket, from Debbie Bliss's *Bright Knits for Kids*. It's a really lovely thing. If you are a new knitter, or the type who feels a little woozy with color projects, then read this slowly, perhaps while sitting down.

Ten colors. Cotton. Intarsia.

Now I'm an experienced knitter, but even the surest of needle persons knows his or her limits, and while I love the Bird Jacket, those three elements are the bane of my existence. I should have remembered that ten colors is a lot, that I hate weaving in ends, and that intarsia in cotton is a particularly difficult thing for me. I've seen lovely examples, and I bow to knitters who can make intarsia in cotton look even and smooth, but every time I do it, I end up half crazed. For reasons that escape me even now, it takes a superhuman effort for me to end up with something that looks respectable. Cotton makes me curse.

But all of self-knowledge went straight down the tubes in the face of the challenge on the table. He claimed that this sweater was "too hard" for him? Well, without being unkind, from the look of his knitting, he had a point. He claimed that Debbie Bliss should read Elizabeth Zimmermann. He was livid with her for having the gall to put four colors in a row.

"Nobody can do four colors in a row," he claimed angrily. He seemed to feel that Elizabeth's dictum ("two colors in a row") should be a law, not a suggestion.

I murmured supportive things, discussed the benefits of patience, and suggested other strategies for making this work. He was unmoved. He had a hate on for Debbie Bliss, her Bird Jacket, cotton, and knitting in general. His rant only served to motivate me further. After all, I am superknitter, and "It's too hard," and "Nobody can do four colors"—well . . . them's fightin' words.

I gathered up the ten balls, told him that I'd knit it for him, and set him up with an easier color project so he could improve his skills. I was feeling pretty cocky.

I cast on, feeling rather full of myself for (a) rescuing him, (b) being hailed as an all-powerful knitter who can manage the accursed Bird Jacket, and (c) promising him he could have it by his deadline, in two weeks . . .

Which brings us to today.

During the last two weeks I have been brought to my knees by this itty-bitty, ten-color, cotton, intarsia Bird Jacket. Disclaimer: This is not Debbie Bliss's fault. Her pattern is lovely, error-free, and clear. The yarn is great and I still think that Debbie is a wonderful designer.

I do harbor a secret belief that she is somewhere in the world, drinking tea, knitting something in wool, Fair Isle, with two colors to a row, while laughing about the Bird Jacket, because she never intended for anyone actually to try to knit the thing.

I tried to strand parts of it, but there would be long floats along its back, and any attempt to catch the yarn not in use along the back resulted in its peeking through. This meant that there is no way out of the intarsia trap. I had to knit each little section with a separate tiny ball of yarn, resulting in lots of hanging lengths along the row—in one particularly demented row, more than twenty. I only managed to keep the number as low as twenty because I stranded the background color. There are long floats of yarn on the wrong side, but they run along the bottom edge of the sweater, and in a particularly successful fit of denial, I managed to convince myself that little fingers won't get caught in them there.

Now it's finished. Well, the knitting part is finished. Now I have to weave in the ends. All by itself, this is a huge job. No, huge is too simple a word, this in an enormous job, a staggering job. It is almost insurmountable. There are ten colors, all these little motifs (freakin' birds . . . I hate their little two-stitch yellow beaks) and all of these billions of tiny birds with fancy tails are surrounded with four-color stars and interspersed with many, many two-row stripes. Guess how many ends to weave in?

No, I mean it. . . . Guess.

Now double your guess . . . heck, just for fun, triple it.

Now read this number. (Again, you faint of heart might want to take a couple of deep breaths or sit down or something.)

Two hundred and eighty-eight.

That's right, 288 ends. Remember, it's only a tiny thing, size one year, so 288 ends means that the wrong side resembles a shag carpet.

I don't know if I can do it. I really don't. Each end needs to be woven in such a way that the right side isn't disrupted (remember that this is cotton, not lovely forgiving wool), and secured in a way that it will neither peek through the (you may insert the expletive of your choice here) cotton, nor work its way free, as it's slippery to boot.

I know what you are thinking. You are thinking that I should have knit them in as I went, and I thought of that, but when I tried it, the end peeked through the damned cotton on the right side, and I just couldn't live with the look.

All I keep thinking is that Debbie Bliss is mean, or crazy, or both.

I suppose that there is also the possibility that she is a far more skilled knitter than I am, and expects a higher level of competence and commitment than a mere mortal such as myself possesses, but it doesn't seem likely.

I am sitting here (frankly, I'm typing to avoid weaving in ends) when I decided to read through to the end of the pattern. Maybe the last line is something like "When you are finished you will have 288 ends. Sorry about that." Or, "See page 67 for instructions on how to avoid having 288 ends." Or, "Whatever you do . . . don't try to weave in these ends . . . it's sheer folly and nobody does it." Or, "Trim the 288 ends to an even length, as the "shag" interior is part of the sweater's charm." Or, "Invoke the spell on page 45 to have your ends woven in magically as you sleep."

But no, nothing. In fact, just to add insult to injury, the last line actually reads . . .

"Work 1 round of dc around outside edge, working 2 dc together in each corner, ss in first dc. Do not turn. Work 1 round or backward dc (dc worked from left to right)."

After a moment of nauseating shock, I have no choice but to accept the truth.

These are not knitting instructions. This is CROCHET.

I hereby admit publicly that I've been beaten.

Freakin' birds.

Operation: Cast On

*A*ttention, knitters! The time is almost at hand. There are now fifty million knitters in North America with more joining us every day. The popularity of knitting is increasing moment by moment. If we are to succeed in our plan to take over the world, we must not let our guard down.

Remember that there are those who do not understand our vision. They care nothing for "Wool Access" and they are unmoved by the words "Yarn Subsidy." Some of these people may live in your neighborhood or even in your home. Watch out for those individuals who would attempt to thwart our cause by limiting your stash or time to knit. Do not let them distract you with their tricks. Most often they try schemes like *jobs, marriage,* and *romance.* Resist.

I have devised a series of tests to allow us to quietly identify each other, even outside our headquarters (code name: yarn store). These tests can also be used to spot "potential knitters," thus reducing the amount of time wasted on trying to convert those who are not yet ready to join their brothers and sisters in yarn. These tests are simple and reasonably conclusive.

1. Give the suspected knitter a handknit sweater. Those who knit, or are destined to become knitters, will turn the garment inside out to look at the making up and the weaving in of ends. They will do this instinctively. Those who lack the knitting gene will admire only the outside of the sweater.

2. Surreptitiously place several skeins of wool in a variety of colors on an accessible surface. Observe the response of the subject to the yarn stimuli. Those who knit will be unable to walk past the yarn. They will fondle, stroke, and possibly smell the skeins before continuing on their way. Should you encounter a subject who arranges the skeins by colorway or who attempts to steal the wool, quickly make contact, as this is likely to be a plan supervisor or "master knitter."

3. Hide some yarn in the location to be tested. Those who are knit-sympathetic will be inexplicably drawn to the area of the hidden yarn. To confirm their tendencies, approach the subjects and invite them into another room. Those called to the fiber arts will resist leaving the room with the secreted yarn, even if promised cake to do so.

If you believe that you have identified a member of our cause, use the password "circular needle." If the person is indeed a member of the revolution, he or she will reflexively voice an extremely strong opinion on this knitting tool. It does not matter if the person adores or utterly detests circular needles; what matters is the passion.

Those who are predisposed toward knitting but have not yet been indoctrinated need to be taught the ways of the needle. Agents in the field have found that "novelty scarves" are inexplicably persuasive. Many young targets can be persuaded to knit if given these trendy yarns.

Catch them, get them going, and suddenly eyelash will no longer be enough. They will need more. They will advance quickly through the ranks of intarsia, Fair Isle, and cable. Those who are not yet ready to accept our cause will simply look at you as though you are out of your mind. Ignore them. Our day will come.

I Can Do That

Sitting in the hospital, waiting for my appointment for a test or two, I knit on my sock to kill the time and anxiety. I'm knitting around on double-pointed needles and I'm working on my plain-vanilla sock pattern. No lace, no cabling, no fancy-pants carrying on at all. I'm not even purling, just working a simple knit stitch round and round and round. It's a complete no-brainer, something I'd expect even brand-new knitters to be able to execute without screeching too much about their lack of skills. A woman approaches me as I sit there, and she watches for a moment before she comments on my work.

"Wow," she says. "That looks complicated. I could never do that. I just don't have the patience for it."

People tell me this all the time. They are simply not cut out for knitting. It's too hard for them. They aren't the type. I've prepared a speech for moments like this. It begins with a statement about the simplicity of knitting, and ends with a two-minute tutorial. I'm about to launch into this speech when I happen to glance at the woman's name tag: DR. SUSAN P. ROGERS. SURGEON, NEUROLOGY DEPARTMENT.

I'm so stunned that it's all I can do to smile in her general direction. In fact, I may not be smiling; I may just be staring at her in quiet stupefaction. She doesn't think she can knit? She's a brain surgeon! A freakin' brain surgeon who doesn't think she has the skills or patience to knit? I was speechless. I'm a writer, I'm basically unemployable, and I can knit. How can someone who has one of the most complicated, tedious, and scary jobs in the world think that knitting would be beyond her? The woman uses microscopic instruments to play around with human brains for a job, but she thinks that my tinkering with two sticks and some string is something she doesn't have the patience for? I find myself hit by a second wave of shock: For the sake of every single one of her patients, I hope she is wrong.

This brain surgeon gets me thinking. I've long believed that anyone can learn to knit. Anyone who wants to, that is. I have not yet formulated a plan to *force* people to knit that is likely to be successful, but the one where I locked resistant people in a freezer filled with yarn and needles has promise, if I can work out the ethical issues.

Still, why does this idea persist that knitters are people with a special aptitude? Sure, there are some knitters who take what's really a mundane act to an art form, and we can't all expect to be like them. But simple knitting? Five-year-old Danish children can manage it. Illiterate people all over the world can knit brilliantly. But not a Canadian brain surgeon?

Knitting is way less complicated than, say, reading and writing, but we expect everybody to be able to do that. Reading is a serious undertaking. A person must be ready to learn, remember, and adeptly use a code of twenty-six symbols (and that's just English) along with the mysterious sounds that each of these symbols represent, and the relationships they have with one another that change the way you decode them. They must be able to manage these symbols in complex strings, putting the code together first into words, then into phrases and sentences. Compared to English, knitting has only two pieces of code, the knit stitch and the purl stitch, and all the knitting in the world is varying these two actions. If you only ever learned these two pieces of knitting code, you could make a really fine blanket.

English also has all these crazy rules, and we inflict the need to know them on mere children. Why, you need to know about words such as "which" and "witch" and that you can "while away" your time "while" knitting. In English, you park in a driveway, drive on a parkway, and "double parking" is really just stopping in the street and doesn't involve parking at all, unless you mean that stopping is parking and that parking is never the verb that means "going to the park" even if you are going to sit down when you get there, thus parking yourself to knit for a spell. It's complicated. Really complicated. And yet the world is full of people who read and write English proficiently, perhaps even know a couple of other languages. But they will still look you in the eye and tell you that even though they have a Ph.D. in philosophy, have learned Chinese for a trip to the Orient, or are a freakin' *brain surgeon* that they simply couldn't learn to knit.

I think it's all about attitude. Knitting is only complex if you have already made up your mind that it is. Historically speaking, there wasn't any room for "It's too hard" in knitting. Virtually every child was expected to knit in medieval England, turning out stockings that would have impressed the heck out of the brain surgeon. In Latvia, a girl needed to knit a multitude of pairs of mittens for her dowry, and the history of Latvia isn't filled with tales of women who remained spinsters to their sad and lonely deaths, all because they weren't the knitting sort of girl. You knit. Period. It was assumed, just as we assume with reading and writing now, that just about everyone is capable of the act.

A while ago I was knitting a sock on the subway when a lady got on and stood next to me. She was wearing a brightly colored dress, and had bags and bags full of shopping. When she spoke to me she had a thick Jamaican accent. She was the very picture of competent powerful womanhood.

"*Look at you! Is that knittin' or crochetin'?*" she demanded in a big loud voice, and she reached over fearlessly to feel the wool dangling from my work.

"It's knitting," I replied, "It's a sock."

"*Well, I'll be damned! How come you got so many needles?* Oh, never mind. . . . You are goin' in a circle, you are *makin' a tube*! Slow down now . . . How does that go? Are you just movin' *dat loop*? No, I see now, you are *wrappin'* the wool around.*"

She was very interested, and her voice was booming. Her voice was, in fact, loud enough that everyone in the subway car was straining to look at what was going on. If I were less polite, I might even say that she was yelling.

"*Look at this!*" she bellowed, tugging on the sleeve of the man standing near her. "It's a sock! *She's knittin' it!*" The man smiled politely at me and then at the sock and looked desperately out of the window at the dark wall rushing by. This woman was clearly ignoring the code of the Toronto rush-hour traveler. You aren't supposed even to speak to other people on the subway, and you certainly don't yell at them about socks and knitting. If she grabbed him again, the man looked like he might get off at the next stop, whether or not it was his right one.

"*Show me what yer doin'!*" she yelled. I knit a stitch or two, showing her how to work it.

I was starting to wonder if she were crazy. I decided that she couldn't be that nuts. If yelling about knitting is one criterion for institutionalization, some of my knitting friends are at risk of being picked up by the men with the huggy coats. I demonstrated for a few more minutes until she got it.

"So you *just makin' loops* in layers, *den it's a sock!*"

She was enchanted. I could tell. Some people are born with a longing for the fiber arts. Others are called to them on a crowded Monday night subway ride. The excitement was plain on the woman's face. I could tell that she was thinking about taking up knitting. I was thrilled. I seemed to have converted someone, and I didn't even need the speech I was going to give the brain surgeon.

She stated her summation with a simple yet joyous eloquence that I envy.

"*Well, shit, girl! I can do that!*"

One Little Sock

*I*t is a little dark in the hospital labor room. A knitter sits in a rocking chair beside the bed. She rocks and knits, rocks and knits, mostly because there is nothing else to fill this moment. The woman in the bed is finally asleep, but even with drugs to help her sleep and numb her contractions she still moans a little with each one.

The knitter pauses in her work and leans forward to the edge of the bed and smoothes the woman's hair. They are alone in the quiet room. She wouldn't dream of being more than an arm's reach away. You never leave the brokenhearted.

The knitter is also a doula, a labor companion, and she has done this a hundred times—sat with a woman in labor. She always knits something for the baby during the quiet waiting times, times while they wait for labor to get interesting or when people are resting, like now. She starts with tiny little socks. They get done pretty quickly. For the fastest labors you might only finish a single sock. If things go on a little, sometimes she gets to knit a hat that matches. Only rarely do things go on long enough that she makes a wee sweater. When women asked about the order of operations and she tells them, "Socks, hat, sweater," they shudder a little. "Not the sweater!" they say. It's pretty upsetting to think that you could be in labor long enough to get a whole outfit. The knitter always laughs and tells them she's a really fast knitter, and that she's sure it will just be socks.

Mothers love having something that was made for the baby while they were having the baby, and they often find the doula's quiet knitting reassuring. They look over during their labor and see her knitting, and they know everything is all right. Who would just sit there if things weren't all right? If she's knitting, then they are okay.

The knitter-doula loves her pager. When it went off this morning, she was so happy and excited that it almost didn't matter that she was going to have to leave her first cup of coffee. There's nothing like waiting for a baby. The beep of a pager sounds so insignificant, but it might as well be trumpets blaring to announce the impending arrival of a whole new human being. Every time the knitter hears it she thinks, "Now we'll get something good," and she scurries off to pick up her wool and needles on the way out the door.

Tonight her wool is soft blue. When she'd arrived at the woman's house earlier that day, the woman had asked her what she had chosen. Blue, even though they think this baby is a daughter. The woman has dark hair and eyes, and the knitter imagines the baby will have them too. Dark brown hair looks pretty with pale blue. Pink would be more traditional, but the knitter and the woman aren't traditionalists.

When she arrived at the woman's house this morning, the knitter put her soft wool yarn and tiny needles on the table and gave the woman a hug. She became the doula, and asked all the questions, filled in forms. The water had broken a little while ago, clear and perfect, and contractions had started shortly after. Everything was exactly as it should be. It would be a long time before it was time to go to the hospital though; things were moving slowly. "Not the sweater, right?" asked the woman. "No, no" laughed the doula-knitter, running her practiced hands over the warm, round belly.

She and this baby had already met. They had played games of "I poke you and you kick me." The baby liked to lie on her right side and deeply resented the doula's friendly poking. The doula knew the baby's body: the lively curve of the bum, little knees, elbows, and heels.

But this time, when she poked, nobody poked back. The doula packed up her knitting.

"We've got to go," she told the woman, and they phoned the hospital for advice. They took the fast way to the hospital, and she comforted the woman with wool, casting on a little sock on the way. It was meant to be a good sign, knitting the sock. No need to panic, no reason to stop knitting. They worried with pale blue wool all the way.

At the hospital, the knitter put away her work again and told the doctor and nurse that they have come because the baby is "quiet." She said this in a way that she hoped meant nothing to the woman and everything to the doctor. "Quiet," she said again.

Suddenly everything went very fast. The gentle knitting was

replaced by monitors, beeps, and ultrasounds, cold things that plug in. The woman and the doula were both badly frightened now. The nurses were impossibly gentle, the doctors impressively kind. The baby was still quiet. There was only bad news, the worst news.

Hours later the whole thing had gotten too cruel. It is a horrible truth that you must finish what you start, even though it seems too sad to do. The doula counseled carefully. They had planned a natural birth, since it would be better for the baby, but now? Now it isn't better. "Ease the pain," she soothed. "It hurts enough."

By then it was late, and the woman was very, very tired. When the medicines worked, she fell asleep. The doula-knitter hoped that she would sleep for a long time, for when she wakes up, it would be sad work.

Now the knitter sits down in the rocking chair. She thinks about it for a little bit, and then she picks up the pale blue yarn and starts back to work on the sock. This will be over long before she knits a sweater; in fact there will probably only be time for this one little sock. The knitter is careful not to knit the sock too long. Nobody is going to grow into it, and she wants the woman to have something just the right size.

Let us call the woman a mother now, for though there is no baby to take home, there once was one. The daughter played poking games and rolled over and heard her mother's voice. Even though the mother will have no child, she will be a mother. This one little sock will be her proof.

What Passes for Perfect

*I*magine for a moment: You are cuddled in your favorite knitting spot, feeling pleased with the progress you have made on your complex project. It's been challenging, and you really are proud of yourself for getting this far. You spread the knitting out on your lap, smooth it with your hands, and start to feel a little smug. You run your fingers down your work. . . . This is a wonderful knitting moment. Then you see it. Down there, right near the bottom, the fourth row. It's a mistake.

How you respond to this exact moment defines your knitting personality.

There are Type A personality knitters out there. They are going to fix every error, every time. Used the wrong color in the second row? They will rip back eighteen inches of complex Fair Isle. I've seen them do it. It boggled my mind. Watching yards of unraveling two ply come out of a sweater is enough to give me nausea. I applaud Type A knitters; I admire them; I wish them well. I know that the search for perfection makes them happy,

But for me, I just know that there is a very fine line between "searching for perfection" and "getting crazy enough to throw myself on a pile of double-pointed needles and hoping for a fatal puncture."

I think about ripping out my work, I really do. But I'm a happy knitter, and I want to stay that way. I have therefore developed several other strategies. If you aren't a Type A knitter, maybe these can make you happy too.

(Warning: If any of these solutions makes you feel light-headed or causes a ringing in your ears, it may be that you do not need to lighten up but are actually a Type A knitter. If so, it is vital that you use Type A solutions or you will hate everything that you knit and not sleep nights at all.)

Problem: Doing the long-tail cast on, you realize that you do not have a long enough tail. You need to cast on 250 stitches, and you are only going to make 246.

Type A solution: Undo the cast on, make a longer tail and cast on again.

My solution: Increase four stitches in the first round/row. No one will ever know. This really isn't going to work if you are casting on 12 stitches, but 250? May my wool be my witness, no one will ever, ever know.

Problem: You discover that your interpretation of the cable chart was . . . umm . . . creative. Twenty rows after the fact, you discover that the traveling stitches to the left of the cable aren't meant to travel at all.

Type A solution: If you are going to do a thing, do it right. Unravel those ten stitches down twenty rows and embark on a process of knitting them back up that requires your pattern, a magnifying glass, natural light, another "refreshment," an hour of your time, and the precision attitude of a neurosurgeon.

My solution: Carefully determine what you did wrong. Write it down. Now, repeat it every time you come to this part of the pattern. Say after me: "I altered the pattern to better reflect my own personal style."

Problem: While knitting the body of a fine-gauge Fair Isle sweater, you discover that you really need to sit in better light/not knit so late/not knit without your glasses because when you move to the light/wake up/put on your glasses, you can see, to your horror, that on the chart you have been following, what you thought were all large dots (dark blue) are actually inter-spersed with small dots (light blue). This means that you have entirely missed the light blue.

Type A solution: Rip out all your work, all the way back to the first insidious little small dot and redo it, meticulously adding the light blue.

My solution: Are you kidding me? Put on your glasses, set the light blue aside for socks, and move on with your life. Eat chocolate if this doesn't feel right. Trust me, you'll get over it.

Problem: While knitting a stegosaurus sweater for your nephew you sort of completely forget to knit in the eyes. Oddly, this rather obvious detail is only discovered during blocking.

Type A solution: Probably rip back the front and reknit, but on a relaxed day; maybe put the eyes in with duplicate stitch.

My solution: Explain to your nephew, using cautiously devised detail and passion, how dinosaurs only developed eyes in the early Cretaceous period.

Problem: While gloating over the gloriously soft and fuzzy mohair stole you knit your sister for Christmas, you notice that the lace on row 2 is wrong.

Type A solution: You run a thread through the row above the error, then snip a thread in the offending row. Draw the mohair painstakingly through, undoing all the stitches in that row. When all the live stitches are exposed, knit down to what would be the cast-on edge and cast off. Pay no attention to the throbbing vein in your forehead.

My solution: Fuzzy stole? How fuzzy? Fuzzy enough to obscure the error? I bet it is. Try squinting.

Need more help rationalizing? Legend has it that in ancient Persia, the famous carpet weavers would deliberately make one error in their rugs. The idea was that "only Allah is perfect." It would be rude to try to compete with God's perfection.

Are you meant to correct every mistake? Is that dropped stitch providence? What about the road not taken? How would your life be different if you didn't fix it? What about the romance of the muse? Imagine for a moment that you use a quick fix instead of a three-hour one . . . Would you catch an earlier bus? Who would be at the bus stop? Perhaps the missing light blue in my sweater is a message. Maybe it's better that way. Maybe these seemingly trivial moments are memos from the divine. Perhaps we have no right to alter the path chosen by the art itself. Let art be for art's sake, move past the practical to the ethereal. I am but a mere mortal not entitled to influence the course of the world. Perhaps what passes for perfect is perfect by itself. I'm not ripping back my sweater; I'm letting it choose its destiny.

Besides, I'm fixing to start some socks.

Veni Vidi Steeki

*T*here is knitting and there is Knitting. Capital-K Knitting is not about making yourself a nice new hat and having fun at it. It's about a lifestyle. It's about trying to learn everything there is to learn about the art of knitting and not being afraid to try things. It's about operating without the fear that your whole life might be sinking into an abyss where only Knitting matters. Capital-K Knitters are a certain sort. I think of a Knitter as a craftsperson or an artisan, perhaps like a master carpenter with years of experience and a broad range of well-honed skills. Imagine calling a carpenter to do all your new woodwork and being told that he doesn't *do* pine and has never framed a window because it looks kinda hard. What if he told you that, frankly, jigsaws give him the willies?

A while ago, I realized that I had a huge gap in my skills when it came to traditional color work. I could get my head around knitting a ten-color sweater; I could rise to the challenge of complex charts. I could even imagine myself weaving in all the ends. But steeks gave me the willies. It was beyond my imagination that you could struggle with all that complexity and then take a pair of scissors to it. To my way of thinking, steeks are a pretty strange idea.

What's a steek? you ask. Let's say you want to make a cardigan. In my sane little world, you knit two sleeves, a back, and two front panels. In steeking, you would instead knit two sleeves and a tube for the body. To make it a cardigan you simply take a nice sharp pair of scissors and cut right up the front; then you cut some armholes to sew the sleeves into as well. Depending on your wool (and level of anxiety, I imagine) you sometimes run a line of machine stitching down the edge of your intended cut, but sometimes, unbelievably, you just pick up a pair of scissors and have at it.

I would never do this. I cannot tell you the aversion I had to this idea. I was happy knitting my sweaters in pieces, not cutting them into pieces. I was willing to keep my dirty little secret. I was chicken. I was a knitter . . . not a Knitter.

I was happy with my nonsteeking position until one day while surfing the net, I came across a reference and a picture of a sweater somebody was knitting. The pattern was called St. Moritz, by Dale of Norway. "Sucker," I thought. I couldn't imagine a sweater that's worth it. It's a very lovely sweater, but it embodied the very things that scared me to death. I forwarded the picture to a friend, with a note that said, "Isn't this beautiful? How long do you think it took to knit?"

I was not going to knit this sweater. No way. Okay, it piqued my interest, but it had steeks. It was clearly Knitting, not knitting, and despite my growing obsession with it, I knew I was not that sort of knitter. Secure in my self-knowledge, I felt that I could safely wander by the Dale of Norway Web site for a better look.

There it was again, St. Moritz. This sweater was seemingly made for me. I loved it. I wasn't going to knit it though. There was a link to "The St. Moritz Sweater Story," but I refused to read it. There's only one thing I liked better than a good sweater, and that's a good sweater story. If the St. Moritz story was interesting, it was only going to feed the obsession, and since I was *not* going to knit this sweater . . . I left the site before I got sucked in.

I heaved a sigh of regret and eyed my knitting. It all seemed so monochrome and pale . . . I've tried colorwork and I don't like it. It didn't go well. I started reasoning it out a little. The last time I tried was years ago. I knew more now, I was a better knitter, and I did colorwork on small things all the time. Maybe I should take the plunge? This was a big decision. St. Moritz was priced like the lovely classic it was, and if I was going to be spending that kind of money on a sweater, I didn't want to rush into it. I caught myself considering my Visa card and realized that I was thinking about knitting this sweater. I jumped back from the edge.

Later, I checked my e-mail. The friend to whom I sent the picture of St. Moritz had answered. She wrote, "You need this sweater." While I liked her attitude (the obsession was developing here) I was still resisting. To ice the cake, she had thoughtfully visited the Dale site, and had cut and pasted the St. Moritz story into her e-mail. I read it, and I was enchanted.

Did I say that I liked a good story? Did I mention that I also loved symbolism? St. Moritz was rife with it. The sweater was named for St. Moritz, Switzerland, where the sun shines 322 days a year. Every element of the sweater represented something. The four languages of the country, the horns of the mountain goat, Swiss chalets, edelweiss flowers, mountains, the sun . . . It was like visiting the Alps. (I've always wanted to visit the Alps.) I found myself sinking deeper and deeper into the charms of this sweater. It was still winter here in Toronto, and all you'd have to do to cast a spell on me is talk about 322 days of sunshine.

Even the steeks were starting to seem reasonable to me. Other knitters do them all the time, right? Stranded colorwork is hugely popular. Why was I out in the cold? I wanted to be a chic stranded-colorwork Knitter . . . I wanted to carry a color in each hand and produce magic. Dale of Norway wasn't just the be-all and end-all; it was just the beginning! There were hundreds of designers out there, all producing beauty like this. That's right! I was getting on the colorwork train and St. Moritz was the first stop. My destiny was clear. This sweater just kept turning up. I was meant to knit it. You betcha . . . here I go, no stopping me now.

I took a deep breath and got a grip. I remembered that I didn't actually know how to do all those things, and that I was about to spend a lot of money on good wool and a decent pattern, which I was promptly going to turn into crap. The fear returned. I turned my back on St. Moritz and Norwegian sweaters and I returned to my e-mail. There is no such thing as destiny.

There was another e-mail from my friend (who, I was beginning to suspect, might not have my best interests in mind when she sent these things). She had spent a little more time investigating the Dale of Norway site and had learned that each of the different colorways available for St. Moritz represents a different element of the Norwegian ski team. Cross-country, downhill, slalom . . .

The one I adored, the one with the natural gray paired with various blues and white—that one is for freestyle.

That was it. I couldn't take anymore. Freestyle is my approach to life. This was a sign.

I decided I would knit St. Moritz, and after that there would be nothing that I could not do. I would carry colors in both hands; I would use those stitch marker thingies; I would organize my charts and mark off completed rows. I would knit a traditional Norwegian sweater, and then I would steek it. When people saw me wearing this sweater they would stop me in the streets and offer me money for it. They would scarcely believe that this sweater was not a dream, never mind that I made it with my own two hands. It would go with my jeans, it would make me look ten years younger. It would be Knitting with a capital K.

It took me 166 days to knit St. Moritz.

Day 1. The book says to cast on 278 stitches, join, and work in the round. I enthusiastically cast on 268 stitches and knit for some ways before noticing. I ripped it back and cast on again, still enthusiastically. I cast on 278 stitches, noting that the pattern doesn't say, "Join, being careful not to twist." Clearly Dale of Norway respects my intelligence. Twenty minutes later it becomes clear that I don't deserve their respect. I curse loudly at the twist in my knitting and rip it back. Third time's the charm. I put my work down triumphantly, with two rounds to show for six hours of knitting.

Day 3. I have finished the hem facing. This is absolutely going to work out. I love this yarn and these colors. This is brilliant. Why didn't I try a Dale sooner?

Day 16. Why didn't I try a Dale sooner? Twelve inches of fine-gauge plain knitting for the body, that's why. I'm starting to understand the psychology of this thing. By the time I get to the scary charts I'm going to actually be grateful for the change. I am no longer concerned with the idea that the charts are going to rob me of my sanity. I know now that intellectually speaking, I will only be "knitting with one needle" (if you know what I mean) when I get there.

Day 25. I have been sucked into the black hole of knitting. I don't understand how this happened but there seems to be a rift in the time-space continuum centered right over this sweater. I knit and knit and knit, round after round after round, and make no progress. This morning the sweater measured eleven inches. I swear that I have knit at least two hundred rounds and the sweater still measures eleven inches.

Day 31. I have ignored the sweater for five days. It is now twelve inches. I don't even begin to understand how that can be possible but I am grateful. Now I start the charts!

Day 45. I made a mistake. I used the wrong blue for two whole rounds. I only noticed when I got to the part with the symbol for the right blue. The thought of ripping this back makes me want to sell my children to raise the cash for a flight to Tahiti.

Day 50. I have decided that I am knitting an "interpretation" of St. Moritz. I'm not ripping back the wrong blue. I am going to make the same mistake on the sleeves so that it looks right.

Day 60. There is no way that anyone can be this stupid. I've knit past the center motif on every row. I get into the rhythm of the pattern and then I just breeze on by the star in the center, then have to tink back, one stitch at a time, and then reknit it with the star in place. I wonder if I would be finished with this sweater by now if every stitch I knit counted.

Day 72. I'm starting to be concerned that all the partying I did in the eighties did more damage than I thought. Very, very carefully, with a great deal of diagramming and math, I have managed to center the back neck shaping of the sweater exactly over the back motif, and the front neck shaping precisely over the right armhole.

Day 75. I have cast off the body. It's pretty impressive. The stranding lies flat. You would never know that my interpretive dance with the colors wasn't intentional. There really are no armholes though.

Day 84. The first sleeve is done, I had to rip it back when I forgot to use the wrong blue to make it match the body.

Day 87. Half of the second sleeve is done.

Day 95. Half of the second sleeve is still done.

Day 121. Half of the second sleeve has been accomplished.

Day 142. Since I can think of no other way to write that I've made no progress on this sweater in fifty-five days it is time to admit that I may be avoiding knitting the second sleeve in an attempt to avoid the steeks. I'm really uncomfortable with the idea of cutting this sweater, but I don't want to openly admit that I'm the kind of chicken knitter who would avoid steeks, so instead I'm avoiding the sleeve. On what planet is it more honorable to avoid the sleeve?

Day 145. I'm working on the sleeve. It seems to be taking a lot longer than the last one, but it's likely because I hear the tolling of the steeks in the background.

Day 151. All hail the mighty knitter!!! I have finished all the pieces. They are lying snugly upstairs drying from blocking. They look wonderful, I love them. I love the colors. I love my knitting. I love how nicely I wove in the ends. I feel like Wonderknitter. When they are done drying, all I have to do is to sew up the shoulders, measure the depth of the sleeves, mark that onto the body, get a pair of sharp scissors and cut up my masterpiece. Am I the only one to whom this plan seems odd? I remain suspicious that this is a cruel Norwegian joke.

Day 153. I am a raving idiot. It's a wonder that I haven't hurt myself. I very carefully measured the sleeve depth, then marked that depth on the body, then with the focus of a diamond cutter sewed 2 rows of machine stitching around the steeks, picked up my scissors, took a deep breath, and looked at the cutting line, blades raised. It was at this precise moment that I looked at the big picture and thought, Wow. Those armholes are deep. *Really* deep. I then did something that was most unlike me. I stopped what I was doing and double-checked my work.

I hold the finished sleeve up to the body. Looks right. On an impulse I hold the other sleeve to the body. A wave of shock passes over me. I hold the two sleeves up against each other to confirm my suspicion. The two sleeves are completely different lengths and widths. Not by a little; by a lot. While I sit on the floor clutching the sleeves and waiting for the blackness around the edges of my vision to go away, I start trying to piece together what must have happened. I know I cast on the right number, so it can't be that I knit two different sizes. The change of length is in the plain part of the sleeve. I lie on the floor with the instructions. Slowly I realize that I've made a bizarre error with the number of increases. Instead of a total of 23 increases, I've apparently made 32, or something like that. I thought that the second sleeve was taking a lot longer than the first one. I'm searching for my perfectly hidden ends so that I can rip this sleeve back, when the enormity of what almost happened hits me. A steeker's worst nightmare: Cutting the steek inches too long. There's no coming back from that one.

Day 157. I ripped back the sleeve and had a do-over. I was feeling pretty good about it until I realized that I was going to have to unpick the machine stitching that I put in. Note: should you ever have to unpick a double row of machine stitches from a hand knit . . . set aside seventeen hours and twenty-three minutes to perform the task. A decent bottle of merlot takes the edge off of the hostility, but does nothing to improve accuracy.

Day 158. I have measured, remeasured, invited independent measurers to oversee my work, and sought help from Internet steekers. I have checked, double-checked, and obsessed about the stitching. I have had a shot of scotch to fortify my steeking will, and I am ready. With God as my witness I swear that I am going to pick up the scissors and cut up this sweater. Tomorrow, or maybe Thursday.

Day 159. I decide that this is a war cry thing, like a sports slogan, "Just steek it." I realize that I may be overobsessing just a little when I overhear my fourteen-year-old daughter tell a friend, "Yeah, I gotta go. My mom's supposed to cut up this sweater, but she's pretty freaked out."

Day 161. I did it. It worked. The sweater didn't unravel, nothing bad happened. It wasn't a cruel sweater-destroying Norwegian joke after all. Armholes, I got them. Now that I think about it, it's a pretty clever way to make a sweater. Maybe I'll start doing all my sweaters like this.

Day 164. Sleeves (of the same size) sewn in. Sewn into the steeks. The steeks I cut. Did I mention that I cut some steeks in this sweater? There has to be someone else to show this to.

Day 165. Picking up stitches for the neck. So close to the finish line . . . this will be the second time I've done the neck. I'm going to contemplate a tattoo that says "Heads are bigger than you think." I'm always picking up too few stitches for necks. (I suppose I *could* try not ignoring the instructions.)

Day 166. It's done. I'm alone in the house. I show the sweater to the cat. The cat does not give me the kind of reaction that I'm looking for. I put it on, but the cat is still not as impressed as I think she should be. I feel like there should be a parade. Cheering, phone calls from other accomplished knitters welcoming me to the club, gifts, certificates of accomplishment. Some kind of plaque to hang on the wall. I knit a Dale of Norway. I followed charts, I knit with two hands. I broke the barrier standing between me and real Knitters.

I have a new motto for the family crest:

Veni, Vidi, Steeki.

I came. I saw. I steeked.

Good Morning, Class

$\mathcal{G}$ood morning, class, and welcome to today's critique of Stephanie's knitting last night. I'm afraid that we have some real issues here, so let's get started. Shall we view the films of last night's knitting?

First, our subject worked on her very attractive intarsia Eeyore blankie, even though the intended recipient is just about to head off to the seventh grade. *(One point given for stick-to-it-iveness.)* Some of you have raised concerns about the reverse side of this blanket and the multitude of ends that intarsia produces. Given that Stephanie has, in the past, simply stuffed a finished item into the back of her closet and pretended that she never knit it rather than deal with weaving in all the ends, I agree that she is a prime candidate for problematic end management.

What's she doing there? What's going on? Oh yes, that's ideal. Stephanie is exhibiting the ability to learn! She has remembered the last time that she did intarsia (I'm sure we all remember that little episode), when she left weaving in each and every single one of the gazillion ends until she was finished, expecting, perhaps, that little elves would come and save her. Then, overwhelmed with the sheer mass of weaving in to do, she suffered a fit of apoplexy and denied all knowledge of the sweater. In fact, our reconnaissance group can confirm that this sweater is still in the back of the closet, although the subject has buried it with sock yarns and a half-finished hat. This time it looks like she is weaving the ends in as she goes. Well, perhaps there is hope for her after all. (*Two points granted for not repeating past mistakes.*)

After working on the blanket for a reasonable length of time, Stephanie decided to move on to socks. This was an excellent choice as her movie selection for the evening was a rather dorky comedy, and visual comedy and intarsia do not mix. Here again, we see real growth as a knitter. (*One point for appropriate project selection.*) As you know, last year at this time, she would have neglected to switch projects and suffered a critical error (like knitting a third ear on poor Eeyore) while attempting to combine chart reading and comedy watching. Always risky. Having finished the first sock of her daughter's pair, she has actually cast on for the second. (*One point for avoiding second sock syndrome.*)

As Stephanie is a little obsessive about having socks that match, she carefully found the proper spot in the self-patterning yarn's repeat and began. (*One point for fussiness.*) Note that it did not take long for her to realize that something was amiss. (*Good catch there . . . two points for paying attention, despite the movie.*) It appeared that she had made an error in selecting the appropriate start point in the yarn. Perplexed, Stephanie promptly ripped back the sock, double-checked the correct starting spot, and began again. *(Two-point deduction for starting again without changing anything. When will she learn that doing the same thing over again will not give you different results?)* She was surprised to discover several rows later that the same problem was recurring. *(One-point deduction for not seeing that coming.)*

Careful examination of the yarn revealed that although she had knit the first sock drawing from the center of the ball, and she had begun the second sock drawing from the center of the ball, the colors were inexplicably appearing in a different order. After ruling out differing dye lots, (good thought), our test subject slowly worked out that in fact the yarn was exactly the same but had been wound into balls at the factory in a different order. *(One point granted for coming up with the answer; two points deducted for calling it sabotage and muttering about conspiracy.)*

Stephanie then decided that what needed to be done here was either to knit from the outside of the ball, which would be inconvenient for her, as much of the center of the ball had been displaced by this early knitting process *(One point deducted for using the phrase "stupid pain in the arse.")* or rewind the ball into the correct self-patterning order. Stephanie retrieved her very fun ball winder, clamped it to the table, and smiled a little smile for figuring out such a good solution. *(One point granted for figuring out a good solution, two deducted for not remembering that Pride goeth before a fall.)* She rewound it at great speed, chuckling to herself at the joy of ball winders. *(We're letting this one go, ball winders are really fun.)*

When she had rewound the yarn, Stephanie located the correct spot to begin her socks and then noted that she had not solved her problem; the yarn remained wound in the wrong order. (*Two points deducted for foul language.*) Class . . . can anyone tell us where Stephanie went wrong? Yes? You in the back . . . Yes, that's right. If one takes the center of a center pull ball, and puts that into the slot on a ball winder (hereafter referred to as the *center* of the ball winder) and winds, then you still have the former center as the current center. Good for you for figuring it out on the first go. (*Three points deducted for Stephanie thinking that rewinding it again center to center would fix this problem, and another one point deducted for foul language, as well as an additional point for what she almost said to Joe when he asked her what the hell she was doing.*)

Eventually, it occurred to Stephanie that if she wanted the inside of the current ball to be on the outside of the next ball, she would have to do something other than rewinding the yarn perpetually from center to center, and she had a major breakthrough (*Two points for finally figuring it out; one point deducted for being, you know . . . "slow."*) and rewound it from the outside to the inside. This final action meant that after a prolonged period of winding she finally was ready to begin her sock. (*One point deducted for casting on the wrong number of stitches when she was ready to continue; however, two points granted for not setting fire to the entire thing when she realized it.*)

Final score: Out of a possible 14, Stephanie scored -3. Tomorrow's class: an examination of the minimum intelligence level required to knit.

My Family, and Other Works in Progress

The Rules

$\mathcal{I}$ like to think of myself as an equal opportunity knitter. I will knit anything . . . well, I'll knit anything once. We will not speak of terrible mistakes with intarsia in cotton, or the decision that lace-weight cabled sweaters were wise. I'll knit anything that I like, and since I like knitting, the world is my oyster. I'm even more flexible than that, since I'll knit anything that someone I like likes. I'll also knit to prove a point or serve a dare. I'll knit almost any object (though I still don't quite see the point of woolly wine bottle covers or condom cozies or willy warmers) and I'll knit just about any color.

But sadly, not all recipients of my woolly love are as free, commodious, or inclusive as I. Instead, they constantly fetter my whims with their own restrictive rules. Color, for instance. Take sage green. This morning I showed my lovely husband, Joe, who is naturally the manliest of men, a fine sage green wool; I was considering it as a possibility for a pair of felted slippers for a male friend. Joe looked at the wool for a fraction of a second and announced that not only would he never wear it, but that it was "a funny green."

Joe is not a good barometer for acceptable manly color-sense. He is firmly embedded at the straight-Newfoundlander-man end of the color sense scale, and it might be that he's not the best guide to what other men might find acceptable. Joe's personal rules for color are as follows: He will wear absolutely any color as long as it is gray, black, dark blue, or brown. Deep murky green may be acceptable if it's so dark as to be indistinguishable as green. White is okay in small doses, but only on certain parts of the body. You'd be as likely to get him into white pants as you would to get him to wear a negligee to a hockey game. Joe will not wear a garment that combines two colors, even if both colors appear on the acceptable color list. Exceptions might be made for subtleties, like black stitching on a gray shirt, but this is pretty dodgy. There is no chance for a Fair Isle sweater within these rules, verily not even stripes. If Joe sees a man wearing even the most conservative gray-on-gray pinstripes, he will giggle to himself and mumble things like "Whoa . . . what's *he* thinking?" Inexplicably, Joe owns and wears a bright yellow raincoat with a silver stripe on it. It's just a little curveball that he throws in there to attempt to keep me confused for the duration of our marriage.

Since Joe operates on the cautious end of the male color scale, I decided I couldn't completely trust him on the appropriateness of sage green. I called my friend Ken. Ken sits firmly on the other end of the what-men-might-wear scale. Ken actually wears color, and in combinations. He has even been known to be a little avant-garde with the color thing. He once owned a pair of very stylish pants in yellow ocher, and he sports T-shirts in colors straight out of the crayon box. Ken owns many striped things and even dares to flaunt the occasional paisley tie. Therefore, seeking some balance in the question of manly color, I phoned Ken. I described my dilemma and the sage green yarn. Ken is a careful thinker, and he asked what I would knit from it. "Slippers," I replied, sure that he'd vindicate my choice. Any man who owns and often wears a kilt (which Joe insists on calling "a skirt") isn't going to shut me down. See? The key to getting the support you want is knowing who to call.

"I dunno about sage green," pondered Ken. "On your feet? Men don't really wear color on their feet. There's a line you don't want to cross with green . . . how dusty is this 'sage'?"

For crying out loud. What is this? It's not really possible that these two men both believed that a pair of sage green slippers could emasculate someone. I know that the time I happily asked Joe what he thought of the "pretty mauve socks" for my brother, I was completely pushing it, but weren't we starting to get a little silly here? It wouldn't even cross my mind to judge a man's worthiness by his casual at-home footwear. I strangle back the urge to say things to Ken like, "Big talk from the man in the skirt," or, "You're probably wearing stripes; what do you know?"

When does this happen to men? At what age do they generate these rules about masculine fashion faux pas? My little nephew Hank is four and he would seem to be completely oblivious about all of this. He once asked me for a pair of pink dragon mittens, since pink is his favorite color. These mittens would replace his mousie mittens, one of which vanished somewhere in between the park and his house. (We were concerned about the winter weather and the fact that the mousie is lonely and likely cold. We took some comfort in knowing that the wee beast is wool [and a mitten] and may therefore be better prepared for his unexpected adventure than a real mouse.) I suggested to broken-hearted Hank that perhaps, simply to prevent the pink dragon mittens from slipping off unaccompanied, I could put a string on them.

The look on Hank's face said it all. The string plan was soundly rejected. Not because he is a big boy, not because strings are demeaning, and certainly not because the presence of a mitten string speaks to a certain lack of faith in his ability to keep a dragon from meeting the same fate as the mouse, but instead . . . get this! Mitten strings (even on a pair of pink dragon mittens) are not "for boys."

It's not just about color either. Gender-based knitting rules apparently extend to texture, style, and fit. My brother is color-blind, and he's the perfect person to help me work out the manly sweater persnickety protocol. I showed him a pattern book full of patterns for men. I think I've ruled out the variables here. He can't reject a pattern because it's not a manly color; he can't tell what color it is. Not just that, but all the sweaters in the book are shown on men, so if anything I'm biasing him toward thinking the sweaters are appropriate. He rejected eight of the ten choices. I learned the following: Cables are manly, but not too many. Too many cables on a sweater and you start running the risk of "fussiness." Ditto Fair Isle. Stitch patterns must travel in straight lines. Anything "curvy" and they start suggesting a certain feminine allure. This curvy rule apparently also applies to very large sweaters, or very large cables. Lacework of any kind was right out, even if the eyelets make a very macho geometric pattern, and in case it occurs to you, my brother was also not fooled by calling it "openwork."

I was also advised that V-necks are a little touchy, and that I'm out of my mind if I think that there is a beefcake use for mohair. Alpaca is perhaps a little soft and drapey, but tweeds and smooth wool yarns got the thumbs-up, as did any stitch pattern that had a name like "moss" or "bark" or "rope." You could swiftly pass over "vine," "leaf," and anything with the merest suggestion of a bobble, should you wish to knit my brother a sweater, and just keep on walking when you get to the bouclé aisle in the yarn shop.

Where does this leave a knitter? I haul out virtually every men's pattern I own, all the books, the magazines, the leaflets, and the stuff I've printed out from the Internet. I pore over them for hours and discover that once you apply all the rules that I've gleaned, out of the hundreds of contenders, there are only a handful that pass muster. I hunt up some yarn, some plain gray wool ("steel" gray, not "dove" gray), and cast on a sweater for Joe, a sweater so plain that I'll likely have to knit it in small chunks to avoid putting myself into a coma. As I cast on the bazillion stitches it will take to go around Joe's forty-eight-inch chest, I think of the final irony. Not only do men want sweaters so plain they could give you narcolepsy, not only do they want them in boring colors without even a little "yarn over" to keep a knitter on her toes, but they also want them in a yarn with no interest. The irony, I think, as I embark on the first of a hundred thousand mind-numbingly monotonous rounds, is not that we knitters are driven to knit for them despite all of this, oh no . . . the final crushing blow is that they are so often, much, much bigger than the knitter.

What She Gave Me

$\mathcal{S}$he was cantankerous, unkind, harsh, ill-tempered, and tidy. (It's the tidy ones that really get to me.) There are lots of other words for the kind of woman she was, but in my family we were discouraged from using that kind of language. We just said that she was "A hard woman to love." That doesn't mean that no one loved her, just that it wasn't the easiest thing to do. She was my grandmother and looking back, I realized that I loved her because she was in my family, because that was the expectation, and because, well, I supposed that at some point it became a force of habit.

I remember a lot about my nana. In my first memory I am very young. My mother tells me I would have been three and a half and my brother was a toddler. We were sleeping over at my nana's house because my parents had somewhere fancy to go. We didn't want to stay. I have a vivid memory of my brother screaming and screaming in the other room for much of the night. My mother tells me that the next morning, when they arrived to pick us up, James was still crying, and my nana said he was "stubborn and a crybaby." It wasn't that she hadn't taken care of us. It wasn't as though she had endangered us or had been awful; she just hadn't answered his cries. It was his bedtime and that was it. She had put him in bed and walked away. No concern for a little guy in a strange place without his mum. She'd closed the door and left.

It was always like that. It was not that she was cruel; she was operating on her own system of rules and balances. We could watch TV, but we weren't allowed to change the channel. (I believe that this is actually the root of my deep-seated and unreasonable loathing for *Coronation Street*.) You could sit on the couch but you had to keep your feet on the floor. She would make you dinner, but it was awful, right down to the spumoni ice cream that she served us. Like everything else, the ice cream was an enigma. She loved her grandchildren and bought ice cream for us when we came, but she wouldn't go all the way and buy ice cream that we liked. It was like her affection for us was an enormous game of "keep-away." My entire childhood there was not one conclusive piece of evidence that she loved me. Hints maybe, but no proof.

Take the knitting. My nana was a professional knitter who worked for a shop. People would come in and choose their pattern and yarn; the shop would then send it out to my nana to knit up. She was very good and very fast. She knit for us too. Incredible things, things I look back at now with awe. Dresses, sweaters, a pleated skirt and sweater set, a pants suit. A pants suit! Can you imagine how long it would take to knit a kid a pants suit? We still have some of the things that she knit and they are technically spectacular. They represent hours and hours and hours of painstaking expert knitting. There is a sweater there that was knit out of fine, fine yarn and I can feel my hands cramp up just looking at it. She had six grandchildren and we were all showered with knitted gifts. That's love isn't it? You look at all that knitting and finally say, "Aha!" There's the proof. No one would spend that much time on knitting for you if she didn't love you. Knitting an entire wardrobe for a grandchild must be an unqualified expression of adoration and affection—except for one thing.

It's all horrible. Each one of the pieces was a masterwork of knitting skill, an homage to breathtaking ability with the needle, a veritable tribute to dexterity— and each one of them was so unbelievably ugly and uncomfortable that you'd wonder if she wasn't out to punish us. They were the stuff of nightmares. If the color was good, the neck would choke you; if the neck was good, the color was so bad that you would wonder where she bought yarn that surprising. If the color wasn't too bad and the style was okay, then you could be assured it was four sizes too small. There was always something.

I remember getting a birthday present at her house. It was wrapped in pink paper with a ribbon and a bow and I still can feel the tickly feeling in my stomach as I unwrapped it. The anticipation, the hopefulness! A dolly? A set of books? My grand-father had made me a dollhouse and I wished more than any-thing for tiny furniture to go in it. Breathlessly I opened the crisp white box inside and lifted the pink tissue paper . . . and there it was. A knitted sweater and skirt made out of scratchy acrylic the exact color of barf. It was covered with cables that looked like stacked hearts and it was the perfect size; it would have been beautiful, it would have been proof of her affection, except that it was the horrible yellow-green-brown color of barf.

That's the way it was with her. There was always a catch, always the moment where you would look at it, then at her, and wonder to yourself why someone would spend hundreds of hours knitting you a birthday present that would make you look like a hairball. She was baffling.

It only got worse. Once I had this stuff, this token of her esteem, which would leave me wondering, "With knitters like this, who needs enemies?" the real horror would begin. *I had to wear it.* My grandmother had knit this uncomfortable scratchy barf-colored sweater and skirt because she loved me, my mother explained. Now, to show her how much I loved her, I would wear it. It was this vicious circle. She knit them because she felt she had to, we wore them because we felt we had to, and quite frankly, I don't think anybody felt the love.

Our relationship never improved. I never liked her and she never liked me, I didn't recall a hug or a kiss, and in fact, I didn't have any sort of evidence that she ever loved me at all, except for one thing.

It was summertime, and I sat in the warm, quiet rose garden in her backyard, under a willow at the side of the yard in a wooden lawn chair. I remember that my feet didn't touch the ground. Even now, more than thirty years later, I can remember the exact details of everything around me. I'm wearing a blue dress, and my nana is beside me and her dress is white and green, one of those Sears catalog housedresses with no waist. In my lap is a ball of yellow yarn and in my hands are cream-colored plastic needles, and I am knitting for the very first time. I remember every moment. I remember wrapping the yellow yarn around, bringing the needle through the loop, and the thrill of dropping the old loop off. There was something about it that was immediately right—instantly satisfying and spiritually moving. I was taking one thing and turning it into another. It was magic, it was orderly, and it was the first time in my life that I felt a sense of mature accomplishment. I was four, and I was *making something*. I felt powerful. I remember those moments the way that I've heard other people speak of moments of religious epiphany. When I finished a whole row of knitting, I proudly laid the work on my lap and looked up at my nana. "You missed a stitch," she said, and showed me the one. "Keep going." And with that, she went into the house.

Well, I kept going. It's a long time now since I gave up trying to figure my grandmother out, a long time since I stopped wearing barf-colored sweaters in a futile attempt to make her love me or to make myself feel what I was supposed to. It's been a long, long time since I accepted that not every grandmother bakes cookies, tucks you in, and is soothing, loving joy. Now, long after that "hard to love woman" is dead, my whole house is full of knitting and yarn and needles that give me so much happiness that I occasionally (well, maybe more often than that) wonder if I'm normal. The irony is not lost on me that a woman with whom I shared only mutual dislike, a woman whom I loved for no good reason I can think of, and who never once did anything that made me feel completely accepted, now has a legacy all over my house. I wonder then, if her love was some strange genetic thing, like baldness or being nearsighted, and it was there and real and undeniable, but like chromosomes, it was invisible to the naked eye and that like baldness, it simply skipped a generation.

My grandmother's love for me and the proof I always wanted is finally something that I can see, as I fold the soft green sweater, knit with the stitches she taught me, into a box for my daughter's birthday. It turns out that she gave me one lasting, invaluable gift, after all.

Ten Ways to Anger a Knitter

$\mathcal{T}$en quick and easy ways to make a knitter angry:

1. Consistently refer to her work as a "cute hobby."

2. When the knitter shows you a Shetland shawl she knit from handspun yarn that took 264 hours of her life to produce and will be an heirloom that her great-great grandchildren will be wrapped in on the days of their birth, say, "I saw one just like this at Wal-Mart!"

3. On every journey you take with your knitter, make a point of driving by yarn shops but make sure you don't have time to stop. (This works especially well if there is a sale on.)

4. Shrink something.

5. Tell her that you don't know why she knits socks, that it seems silly when they are only $10 for five pairs and they're just as good.

6. Tell the knitter that you are sorry, but you really *can't* feel a difference between cashmere and acrylic.

7. Tell her that you aren't the sort of person who could learn to knit, since you "can't just sit there for hours."

8. Quietly take one out of every set of four double-pointed needles that she has and put them down the side of the couch. (You can't convince me that you aren't doing this already.)

9. If you are a child, grow faster than your knitter can knit. Requesting intricate sweaters and then refusing to wear them is also highly effective.

10. Try to ban knitting during TV time, because the clicking of the needles annoys you.

This Makes More Sense

ℐ have uncovered a plot. For years I have surmised that there was something going on. I didn't share my suspicions with other knitters since I was worried about causing mass panic without being confident of the facts. I have now gathered enough evidence to share the following with you.

It would appear that a group I have named TAKE (Team Against Knitting Enjoyment) is active in my household. I am writing to warn you in case a similar team is operating in your house too. Some of you may be unfamiliar with TAKE, but most of you will either have had personal experiences or know a victim of its baby-led splinter group TAPES (Team Against Parents Experiencing Sleep). I have established that TAKE has four operatives inside my household, and has definitely infiltrated my friendships and extended family.

TAKE is insidious and will stop at nothing to keep you from knitting. Some of their more advanced agents will spend years insinuating themselves your life, even living with you, in order to lull you into their antiknitting web. Some agents are small and innocent-looking, posing as mere children; even your own off-spring may be suspect. These tiny charming agents can disrupt many, many hours of knitting time. Do not allow their friendly manner and cute ways to lull you into a false sense of security.

Be alert to the following clues that TAKE may be active in your home:

The ringleader is the trickiest. This advanced agent appears unafraid to invest years of his or her own life maneuvering into a position to spoil your knitting enjoyment, dating you for a pro-longed period of time or even entering into unions such as mar-riage to ensure a position of influence. He or she may even appear to support you in your desire to knit, softening you up by calling you "dear" or "honey," and perhaps saying things like, "What are you knitting? That's really nice." He or she may even seem to take your side against the other agents, saying, "Go play outside, kids, your mom is trying to knit." Do not be sucked into the web of deceit. Watch for the subtle indications that this per-son is a TAKE member. For example, after sending the children outside, ostensibly so you can concentrate on your knitting, does he or she then interrupt you every two minutes? Expect meals? Need you to find his or her shoes? Attempt to engage in marital relations? This agent will stop at nothing to distract you from your knitting mission.

Other operatives may flatter you or even request knitted objects of your making. Watch out for this insidious phrase: "Wow, Mom, that's really cool; will you make me one?" If you pay close attention to their deeper intentions there will be indications that they are insincere. For example, after requesting a sweater, do they then make it nearly impossible for you to knit it? Common strategies include choosing a yarn you hate using, patterns that are outrageously expensive or out of print, bizarre fitting requests, or color choices that may actually cause permanent brain damage to the knitter. A classic example would be a child (read: operative) who would like an unreasonably complex Aran sweater knit out of acrylic in a neon variegated colorway, with the neckline adjusted so it isn't "choky." Other operatives may catch the flu, lose their mittens, or pester you with requests for homework help. The smallest of these agents is the most effective, especially those weighing less than twenty pounds, since they are willing to get up in the night requesting feeding or comfort, thereby making you too tired to knit. Realistically, these small operatives have less effectiveness than the ringleader, since they must eventually "grow up" and move out of the house. Be aware that while this would appear to solve the problem, in reality they have just completed their training and are moving on to new assignments with other knitters.

If you doubt me, ask yourself this: Does your family claim to have "no problem" with your knitting, but then make unreasonable demands that cut sharply and directly into possible knitting time? This technique is typically used at the precise moments that you sit down to knit. The agents of TAKE, having observed you make yourself comfortable with your knitting, will then attempt to drag you from your task.

Be aware of keywords they may use like "dinner," "laundry," "bills to pay," or "gainful employment." These are simple attempts to distract you from knitting. Don't fall for it.

Other TAKE alerts are simple to spot. Look for gaps in their logic. Do they drive you to the yarn store and then seem surprised or disapproving that you have bought yarn? Do they buy you yarn or support your yarn purchases and then somehow expect closet space? Once you are onto their game, the evidence is everywhere.

The final proof that TAKE is real and rampant is your own stash. Look how much yarn you have. You clearly expect to have way more knitting time than you get. What sane person would buy twenty-four sweater kits if they didn't think there would be time to knit them?

Agents of TAKE, beware, this knitter is on to your game.

Three Blankets

This blanket is a disgrace. It is an abomination of the knitter's art. It is ratty, stained, and used up, and, frankly, it was very badly knit in the first place. Lest you think I am slagging some other poor knitter, I'm the one who knit it. This blanket is so bad that sometimes, when I think about it, I worry that my house will catch fire and that the only thing that will survive the flames is this blanket. Then people will find it and think that this was as good as I ever got—that this was the kind of knitter I was. It terrifies me that this blanket might be my knitting legacy. Whenever this nightmare hits me, I think about throwing the blanket away. But I never do.

I knit the blanket sixteen years ago when I was expecting my first child. I had been knitting for a really long time, but I was a knitter, not a Knitter. I had done scarves and hats and dishcloths, and I'd even done one sweater, although my profound misunderstanding of the true importance of "getting gauge" meant that I had, in the end, knit something that more resembled a sloop's mainsail than a sweater. I had not yet accepted my calling as a Knitter. I still sometimes thought that I might have other hobbies.

Suddenly I was enormously, hugely pregnant with a baby who I was quite sure would never be born, and in those four weeks (two while I waited for my baby due date, and—regrettably—two while I still waited) I knit the blanket. I had seen the lace pattern in a knitting book. Somehow my idea of motherhood included a pretty pink baby in a pretty pink sweater (already successfully knit, except for the overly long arms, for which thankfully I had had a stroke of genius: they developed cuffs), wrapped in a lacy white blanket. I went to the craft shop and found some white yarn. It was the eighties, and it was acrylic. I tell you this because there is a difference between acrylic then and acrylic now. Nowadays, there is such a thing as nice acrylic; then, there was not. I got worsted weight too, even though the pattern called for fingering, because I knew it would make the blanket go faster. At the time, I didn't understand about yarn requirements or about going past your due date. It was a "due date," for crying out loud. Doesn't that mean anything to anyone?

I tried to rush the baby and the blanket. I knit and knit and knit for four weeks. I knit all day long while I waited for something to happen. I knit in the evening while I waited with my husband for something to happen. I even knit a few nights when I was too huge to sleep. My daughter was born the day I finished the white lace blanket and I wrapped her in it and felt proud of the baby and the knitting, as if I had really accomplished something.

Sixteen years later I am both a better mother and a Knitter, and what I thought back then makes me laugh out loud. The idea that I had accomplished something fifteen minutes after my kid was born and I'd knit a crappy acrylic blanket? I had no idea what was going on.

That first blanket knit out of worsted-weight yarn was a weird size. It didn't fit. Because I had used heavier yarn without changing the pattern it had come out really, really wide. Because I had bought the recommended amount of yardage (even though I had changed the yarn) it was also really, really short. It was actually more like a scarf or a wrap. It wouldn't stay wrapped around the baby or fit in the bassinette; it fell out of the sides of the stroller and dragged on the ground. I couldn't get it to behave the way it was supposed to.

The baby was like that too. She didn't fit. I had this idea, this pattern image of the kind of baby I had been making, and she came out all different, just like an unexpected blanket size. She wasn't a pink little baby wrapped in a white blanket. She was usually red-faced and screaming and wrapped in a blanket that wasn't white because it was too damned long and had dragged on the ground again. The baby cried all the time, except when she was eating, and nothing got done. "This wasn't at all what I was expecting," I remember thinking, as I looked at both the baby and the blanket. I had expected both of them to be prettier (and quieter) and cleaner.

If you look at that ratty sixteen-year-old blanket, you will see several mistakes. These are not the sorts of mistakes that you notice only if you are a knitter and fussy. An alien from Saturn, who had never seen knitting before, would point out these mistakes with its long green fingers and question you on them. It's funny that I can see them so clearly now, because at the time I remember thinking that the blanket, like my mothering, was not that bad, just a little rough. Of course, now that I am a real Knitter and a real mother I can't believe that I made it.

If I had the blanket to do over again I would have been more careful. I would have counted my stitches and used markers and taken real care. Somehow though, that first blanket and that first baby weren't about getting it right; I attempted perfection with my every waking moment (of which there were many), but every row and every day quickly disintegrated into just getting through it. I got up, I nursed, I rocked, I walked, I knit. I can see now that I didn't think enough about the pattern, I was too stuck on each individual stitch. I had blinders on, and it was getting through that mattered. There are days when you're a new mother when the day is a success if you manage to get your hair washed.

The border on the blanket is dodgy. There are spots where the edges have come away, or places where I had too many stitches, or too few. I was like that then too. I know that there were days that I cleaned too much, and rocked too little, days that I got the border, the parts of our life that were around the edges, wrong. When you are in the middle of something like that, you forget that it's all going to be a whole. I didn't pay enough attention to the people around the edges—my own mother, who had a wealth of experience, my friends, who could have sympathized. I didn't understand that taking the time to put things around the edges properly would help the whole come together. I worried too much about stupid things and not enough about enjoying myself, my baby, and those things around the edges.

That blanket is on the top shelf of my cupboard, and underneath it are two more baby blankets, one each for my second and third daughters. The second one is quite a bit better than the first one; it's made of better yarn and has fewer mistakes. Even though it's more complicated, it was easier to knit. The second baby was like that. Even though I had two little kids, a bigger house, and a more complicated pattern to accomplish it just seemed to go better. I had improved. The third blanket is beautiful. It's knit of lace weight; the border is seamless and it just flew off the needles, sort of like the third daughter, who just "arrived" one day, to very little fanfare, upset, or acclaim. I didn't make many mistakes that time on either the blanket or the baby. By then I knew about attention to detail, about taking your time, about living to knit another day. I knew that it was worth it to skip a load of laundry to count stitches or read stories and that time spent doing another repeat wasn't a waste but a lovely, enchanting theme.

I've saved all three of the blankets because I hope someday my daughters will take them for their own children, and I'll rock a grandbaby in them. I feel a little bad about the first one. I did such a terrible job. It's so messy and horrible and disappointing that sometimes I think about reknitting it to make it better. Maybe pulling back the yarn and starting over—at least getting it to be a blanket shape. I feel bad that my first daughter got all my messes and endured bad blankets, weird sweaters, and bad days while I learned to how to knit it all together and how to be a mother.

Still, I don't pull the blanket back, I don't reknit it, and I don't throw it away . . . though I do sometimes think about pinning a note to it that says "I got better at this," just in case of that house fire. That misshapen, lumpy, mistake-ridden scarf/blanket is part of our history, a remembrance of those first awkward sleep-deprived and scary times as a Knitter and as a mother, when no matter how hard I tried, it really didn't come together. I've learned that just because I didn't do it perfectly doesn't mean it's worthless. Now I look back with some affection on those days that I knit bad stuff and got dinner on the table at ten because it was all so hard, especially now that I've got a few years of sleeping through the night. I know I made it harder than it had to be. But I've got those later blankets to prove that it was about learning and growing and patience. Every time I think about trashing that pathetic blanket I look at the daughter that I made at the same time. Despite my difficulties, they are both very beautiful.

I keep this blanket because I have this idea, almost a vision. I imagine my first darling daughter is a grown woman, and she has this blanket to wrap awkwardly around her first baby. I imagine that maybe when my firstborn wraps her firstborn in that bedraggled sorry blanket at three o'clock in the morning, when everything seems to be going so wrong, that maybe, just maybe, she won't feel so bad about riding a learning curve. After all, I did that too. The blanket shows you that.

Resister

Dear Designer,

The good news is that I have recently remortgaged my house and can now afford to buy your latest book, though I'm still looking for that second job so I can buy the yarn to go with it.

The bad news is that my eldest daughter has said something horrible. So horrible in fact that I fear for her future. If you are standing up, please sit down. Take a deep breath. Yesterday, as I was trying desperately to occupy the children (when I run the world, it will never rain on days when the kids are home from school), I pulled out your latest book, AbFab Projects for Pubescent Purlers, in an attempt to occupy the dear little souls. The youngest two picked out projects, but when I asked my fifteen-year-old daughter what she would like to knit she looked me in the eye and said, "Mom, I don't want to knit. It's boring."

I can scarcely believe this has happened. I really felt that simply by carrying my DNA she would knit. All my children knit. This must be some form of teenaged rebellion, right? Boring? Knitting isn't boring. Knitting is very interesting (I told her), knitting is good for your mind. Knitting restores order to a troubled psyche. She's a teenager, that's got to be helpful, right? Knitting at its best is absolutely gripping. At its worst knitting is meditative, perhaps, but never boring.

Maybe sometimes the plain bits can wear on you a little. I admit that the second sock of a pair can take inner fortitude. I also admit that on occasion the really big stuff, like blankets, or sweaters for enormous men can seem a bit monotonous, but that's not what's happening here. We are talking about the dear little heart complaining that the entire experience of knitting, even the act of contemplating or casting on a project is "boring." All I could do was stare at her.

I fear for her future, I really do. If knitting is "boring" then what's it going to take to hold her interest? Hitchhiking? Spearheading a revolution? Dropping acid? (Do kids still drop acid? That's something I should probably find out, now that my very own flesh and blood is talking about not knitting.) It's a slippery slope, I tell you. First you tell your mother that knitting is "boring" and next something horrible has happened, like drug addiction, not folding your laundry, or (God forbid!) deciding wool is "itchy."

Ms. Daring Designer, since you are the foremost knitting authority in the world right now and since it says right on the back of your book that your patterns are "too funky for any kid to resist," I ask you: What's a mother to do with a resister?

Yours truly,
Stephanie

Parents and Knitters

$\mathcal{T}$he top ten ways why being a parent is like being a knitter:

1. You have to work on something for a really long time before you know if it's going to be okay.

2. They both involve an act of creation involving common materials, easily found around the home.

3. Both knitting and parenting are more pleasant if you have the occasional glass of wine, but go right down the drain if you start up with a lot of tequila or shooters.

4. With either one, you can start with all the right materials, use all the best reference books available, really apply yourself, and still get completely unexpected results.

5. No matter whether you decided to become a parent or a knitter, you are still going to end up with something you have to hand wash.

6. Parents and knitters both have to learn new things all the time, mostly so that they can give someone else something.

7. Both activities are about tension. In knitting, the knitter has control of the amount of tension on the object in progress. In parenting, the opposite is true.

8. No matter how much time you spend at knitting or parenting, you are still going to wish you could spend all your time at it. Which is odd, since both activities are occasionally frustrating enough that you want to gnaw your own arm off.

9. Knitting and parenting are both about endurance. Most of the time it's just mundane repetitive labor, until one day, you realize you're actually making something sort of neat.

10. One day, you will wake up and realize that you are spending hours and hours working at something that is costing you a fortune, won't ever pay the bills, creates laundry and clutters up your house, and won't ever really be finished . . . and the only thing you will think about it is that you can't wait to get home and do more.

Is This a Test?

$\mathcal{I}$f it is true, and I really believe that it is, that knitting is a soothing force in the world and that the liberal application of yarn can ease any day, then today would be a time when I tested it.

2:47 I have been on call to go to the birth of a baby for almost three weeks. The baby is a week overdue, and the mother lives about an hour from here, so I've got some concerns about getting there quickly when the baby finally starts to come. My birth bag is packed and I've chosen the project that I'll knit while I'm at the hospital. I'm very, very ready to go and maybe a little jumpy, so when my pager goes off at 2:47, I ricochet out of bed, smash my head on the dresser, and try to read my pager as I jam my legs into my jeans. Of course I can't read it in the dark. Only one baby is due, and only my clients use my pager. I don't want to wake Joe, so I ram my noisy pager into my pocket, pull a sweatshirt over my head, and leave the bedroom with mismatched (but hand-knit) socks. I brush my teeth while mentally running through my checklist. Someone to watch the kids, food in the fridge, other commitments to cancel . . . I run down the stairs and note the time, only two minutes have elapsed. I am a star.

2:51 I can't find the phone to return the page. I find my knitting and client file while I am looking, and after several moments of deepening panic (during which it doesn't occur to me to use the other phone), I locate the cordless phone in the basement on top of the dryer. Its battery is completely dead. This is nobody's fault but my own. The fact that the phone was on the dryer means that it was me who left it there. I can be quite certain about this because nobody else in the house even knows where the dryer is.

2:55 I run to the other phone, putting my bag by the door as I go and stringing together expletives. I reach into my pocket, pull out my pager to dial back the number and . . .

It is a 1-800 number. It is pager spam. I am up, dressed, and at my front door at 2:55 in the morning for pager advertising spam.

3:00 I am back in bed, delirious and exhausted but too enraged to sleep. I lie there for quite some time imagining revenge fantasies and composing long and hostile speeches that I will give to the pager people when day breaks.

5:30 Megan's alarm clock goes off. I stagger into her room to shut it off when she doesn't. Megan offers no explanation for why her alarm is set for 5:30, but does ask me why I am sleep-ing topless in a pair of jeans. I have no answer. On the way out of the room I step in an art project that Sam left on the floor and I hop to the bathroom to wash the wet paint off my foot.

5:40 Sam's alarm reports loudly. Megan shuts it off. I try to sleep, but am jolted awake by the thought that the children clearly had some kind of activity planned between 5:30 and 5:40 that was important enough to have a double alarm system.

6:15 The cat wakes me up by licking my nose. I lock the cat out of the bedroom. Nose licking will not be tolerated.

6:27 I let the cat in. It turns out that I would rather have nose licking than incessant cat whining. I am feeling increasingly unloved.

7:30 My alarm goes off. I get up (and hit my head on the dresser again . . . I swear in the name of all things woolly that Joe is moving it around while I'm out of the bed). I rouse the chil-dren and go to the kitchen to start coffee and school lunches. I notice that someone has left the milk out overnight, making cold cereal impossible, so I start oatmeal.

7:34 While beginning to make sandwiches, I see that the bread has been gnawed by a mouse (likely while the cat was lick-ing my nose). I resist the urge to use the bread anyway and make pita pizzas for the girls to take to school. As I put them in the oven I notice that I'm thinking about leaving. I don't know where on earth I would go, but I'm thinking about leaving.

7:45 Note to the Toronto Public School Board: I am as big a hockey fan as anybody. It turns my little Canadian crank that our women's hockey team kicked American arse. If, however, you decide to have a "Red and White Day" to celebrate, I would like you to send some kind of note home so that I get more than twenty minutes to clothe an enthusiastic ten-year-old girl who will not accept compromises (like cream and burgundy) in red and white clothing.

8:01 Locate Sam's red pants in Megan's drawer. Spend five minutes breaking up the fight that ensues. Deal with Megan's emotional reaction to Sam's accusation of pants theft. Deal with Sam's emotional reaction to Megan's denial.

8:11 After defusing the situation, I decide not to tell the children that it was probably me committing laundry error. I remind the children that when it comes to misplaced laundry, ownership is not nine-tenths of the law. Feel briefly guilty for that, but am distracted by the smoke alarm.

8:12 Remove immolated pita pizzas from oven. Curse loudly. Curse even more loudly when I notice that there are pita pizzas on the counter that I made last night before I went to bed. Weep a little.

8:17 Amanda leaves. Note that she forgot her lunch, chase her down the street. Return home, note that she forgot her sheet music for orchestra, chase her even further down the street.

8:23 Amanda is back. She tells me that it is "Striped Sock Day" at her school. I resist the urge to choke her with a pair of striped socks, and instead hand them to her without comment. I decide that it is cruel to have high schools declare a different spirit day than elementary schools. I make a mental note to send viciously worded e-mail to my Member of Parliament later in the day addressing this very issue.

8:25 In a preemptive strike, I ask Megan (who goes to middle school and therefore completes my "three children/three schedules" set) if there is any sort of *"day"* that I should know about. Red and white? Socks? Waffles? Smile to self when Megan replies, "Screw it."

8:30 Walk Sam to school. Feel a thrill of success when I manage to avoid a PTA type who looks like she needs a volunteer . . . (I actually like this lady, but I'm antisocial before coffee.) Then I accidentally run myself into a lowhanging tree branch while fleeing from her. (Subtle. I'm sure she never saw me.)

8:40 Return home. Get my coffee and sit to knit, relieved that the worst is over. Reach for my knitting pattern and discover that the cat has exacted her revenge for being locked out of the bedroom (however briefly) by depositing a hairball on my pattern notes. They are illegible, which is really just fine, because there is absolutely no way that I am even entertaining a suggestion of how to wash cat puke off a pattern. We'll just call it a loss. I reach for my sock in progress instead and drink coffee, glorious brown elixir of life.

9:00 Spend a few minutes peacefully working around and around on my knitting, reflecting that there are really very few things in the world as peaceful, predictable, and worthwhile as turning a ball of yarn into a pair of socks with only coffee for company. I feel the trials I've endured since 2:47 A.M. slip away as the yarn slides between my fingers, forming reliable stitch after stitch. Knitting, they say, lowers blood pressure, relieves stress, and can be a form of active meditation, and I really believe it. This is the first time that I've felt relaxed all morning.

I believe every moment of it, until 9:05.

When my pager goes off.

DPN

This is getting stupid," said Joe. I glared at him with white-hot fury and resisted the urge to say something completely sarcastic in return. I'd been married long enough to know that good relationships depend just as much on what doesn't get said as on what does. There are these moments when you have a choice about what you say to your spouse. You can choose to say something like "Really, Joe? Really? You freaking think so?" or you can choose to say nothing. Given that what was going down in our driveway had passed "getting stupid" about an hour before Joe's comment, I decided that keeping my mouth shut was probably much, much better. The situation was now officially stupid; in fact, it was way past stupid and cruising at a thousand miles an hour toward moronic. It would soon reach unprecedented levels of ludicrous.

The stupidity in the driveway was the kind of stupidity that my children would tell their children about, and their children would pass the story down through generations upon generations. I knew perfectly well that I was giving my children ammunition for those times when people began telling stories that start, "And you think *your* mom was wacko?" I could feel the stupid, but I couldn't stop myself.

I was crawling around the backseat of a rental car. I had been crawling around the inside of the car for over an hour, looking for a lost double-pointed needle. I *knew* it was there. We had just returned from a long car trip, and I had been knitting all the way. Six hours in the car: I knit the whole time and I had all four needles. When we got back to Toronto, we decided that since we had a little time to spare, we would drop our daughters and our luggage off at the house and then drive over and return the rental car before they charged us for an extra day. It was a great plan . . . until I noticed, as I got out of the car, that I had only three needles.

It seemed like a simple problem. When I was in the car I had four needles. Now, without leaving the car, I had three. Ergo, the missing needle must be in the car. Could anything be more obvious?

When I first noticed that the needle was missing, there was absolutely no indication that this was going to get stupid. I checked my knitting bag. I checked my purse. I checked the car floor. Then I got out of the car and checked my seat. Nothing. I rechecked all of those places and then got down on my knees on the sidewalk and looked under the seat. Nothing. I started to think creatively. In the map slot on the side of the door? No. Maybe the needle was on my lap, and when I stood up to get out of the car, it fell on the road. I got out of the car and looked on the curb and in the gutter. Two of my neighbors walked by and said hi to Joe as I flattened myself on the sidewalk so that I could see under the car. They didn't say anything to me. This should have been my first hint that things were getting stupid.

Joe stood by the front door watching me grovel on the sidewalk. I could see him trying to weigh his options. Did he have a better chance of returning the rental car on time if he suggested that I let the needle go (thus possibly provoking a fight) or if he took the needle loss seriously and helped me try and find it (thus condoning, and perhaps furthering, my insane behavior)? Joe decided to split the difference: He helped me look for the needle while suggesting I let go. "Maybe it's stuck in your clothes?" he suggested. "Maybe it stuck on you for a few moments and then fell out, like, over here?" Joe walked the route I took from the car to the house.

"Maybe," I said, crawling behind him. It's a 2-millimeter needle. I wasn't going to find it unless I stuck close to the ground. "Maybe it's in this crack?" I squinted down the crevice between the step and the porch.

"That would be bad luck."

"Yeah," I said, still lying on the ground, peering down into the crack trying to see into the tiny blackness.

"You might not get it back if it's in there," Joe offered. "Maybe we could just return the car and look in the crack when we get back? I could get the magnet. I'd help you, you know, after we return the car."

I turned my head and looked at him. He wasn't getting this at all. The needle might be in the car. If we returned the car, I'd never get the needle back. *Never.*

I loved those needles. They are super sharp aluminum needles, bright blue. I understand that they're commonplace in the United States, but here in Canada, they are rare and special. It's not that they are the best needles in the world—we aren't talking $20 Addis Turbo here. When you first get them the tips aren't completely smooth, and after a while the blue rubs off the tips and they can get a bit rough. But the needle that the rental car had eaten was in the perfect middle stage. I'd nursed it through its imperfect infancy and now it had at least a couple of socks left in it before it was past its prime. I loved it. It was mine. Besides, it was part of a set of four. If I lost one, the other three were useless.

I looked at Joe as if he had two heads. He'd lived with a knitter for this long and now he had suggested that I just give up on the needle? The dude could forget returning the rental car until I got my needle back. I shot him a look that I hoped expressed this sentiment. I'm pretty sure that he got the message, since he started to help me look again.

"Are you sure it's not in your purse?" Joe tried to think. (He also tried to hold a conversation with me that didn't reflect his belief that I was a ripping lunatic. I appreciated that.) "I know you didn't put the sock in your purse but maybe the needle was on your lap and when you were getting out of the car it fell off your lap into your purse?" Joe looked so hopeful that I didn't have the heart to tell him that I'd already practically shredded my purse. I began to check it again, dumping the entire contents onto the sidewalk. Joe started to go over the car again. As he yanked the floor mats free and I scattered my belongings, he tried again.

"Steph, if the car isn't back in half an hour it will cost fifty dollars. Can we agree that we should return the car before it costs fifty dollars?"

"Keep looking, Joe."

"Steph . . ."

"It's one of my blue ones. Keep looking."

We searched in silence for a little while. Then our neighbor emerged from his house.

"Hi, guys, whatcha lose?"

"Steph's lost a knitting needle and she doesn't want to return the rental until she finds it." Joe's voice was beginning to have a little edge of bitterness, and I resented it. He could just have said that I was looking for a needle. He didn't need to drag the whole rental thing into it . . . The neighbor looked for a while, but when I suggested that perhaps we needed to get some tools to remove the seats of the rental car to look properly, he remembered he had a dentist appointment he had to start brushing his teeth for. The vague air of bitterness that Joe had begun to exude was becoming stronger. His brow was furrowed, and he kept checking his watch.

"Steph, in twenty minutes they are going to charge us fifty dollars."

I pretended that I couldn't hear him because my head was under the backseat of the car.

"Steph?" For the love of wool. He wasn't going to give up.

"Joe, it's one of my favorite needles. I want it, I know it is here and I'm having it. There's just no stinking way that I'm leaving it behind."

"I thought the green ones were your favorites? Just last week you said that the green ones were the best you ever had. You're just saying that the blue ones are your favorites because that's the one that's missing." He was practically gritting his teeth while he looked through the luggage again. I resisted the urge to sigh. I am *so* misunderstood as an artist.

"The green ones were good last week, then they got old. Now the blue ones are my favorites. For crying out loud, Joe, if something of yours was lost we wouldn't even be talking about it." This was a stupid thing to say. If I have learned one thing about marital discord it is that one must never, ever attempt to make equivalent arguments. I know (and you know) that if Joe had lost his favorite whatchamacallit in the car, he would be flipping out and we would have gotten the tools out a long time ago. We would have the car up on jacks. The children would be searching with flashlights. The tooth-brushing neighbor would be out with a high-end metal detector and other neighborhood men would have stood around offering support and suggestions. Somebody would have offered to make a chart and grid system for car search effectiveness and another guy would have brought beer. If I suggested in the middle of this testosterone-driven little party that maybe, just maybe, we should stop looking for his beloved possession because the car had to be returned, thus ensuring that Joe would never, ever be able to recover his thingie, he would have gone absolutely berserk about my lack of support and understanding. This, however, is not what Joe believes. Joe believes—I can tell by the way the tops of his ears were getting really, really red—that he would walk away, calmly saying things like "never mind" or "what's done is done" or that incredibly annoying "easy come, easy go," and then return the rental with an air of serenity, coolly kissing off whatever it was that the car had sucked into the seventh dimension.

Joe glowered at me with pent-up wrath while I ripped the floor mats out of the car for the forty-third time. I admit it: I was none too calm myself. With the simmering rage of a normally kind and decent man who had been pushed to the edge of sanity by his unreasonable obsessive wife, he made a last desperate (if hostile) plea.

"Stephanie" (note the strategic use of my full name), "in approximately thirteen minutes your one-dollar needle is going to cost us FIFTY DOLLARS. It is time to go. Ask yourself: Should your priority be a silly one-dollar knitting needle or a FIFTY-DOLLAR rental car! You cannot be this crazy!"

That did it. I'd had it. Crazy? Didn't he know that I could already feel the craziness? I hurled the mat back into the car and whipped around to tell him that this was not about priorities or logic. Not one little bit. I had a hundred double-pointed needles in the house not more than forty feet from us, and he shouldn't call my sock needles "silly" because they kept churning out his precious hand-knit socks. It had nothing to do with the arbitrary dollar value he'd assigned to the missing needle or his precious stinking rental car. This, this was about the principle of the thing. Knitting needles do not disappear. I know for a fact, a *fact,* that the needle had to be here somewhere and moreover, dammit, this was about decency, perseverance, taking a stand and not giving up. There was no way I was giving the car the satisfaction of stealing my stuff. I wanted my needle back, and I'd pay the fifty dollars or however much it was. This was my special, blue, 2-millimeter sock needle, and I was, I swear it, going to get the thing back from this godforsaken thieving car.

This was what I intended to say to Joe as I whipped around sharply in the war zone that was once our driveway. But even as I opened my mouth to let go of all the pent-up stupid-and-crazy, a small, blue, 2-millimeter, double-pointed knitting needle, which had apparently been tucked behind my ear, disentangled itself from my voluminous curls, flew through the air, glinted in the sunshine, and then tinkled audibly onto the sidewalk between us.

I took a deep breath and looked at it. Joe exhaled and looked at it. Then I bent over, picked it up as humbly as I could, and reseated myself in the car.

"Let's go."

acknowledgments

I would forever regret it if I did not extend my deepest thanks to:

Andrews McMeel Publishing in general, and specifically my editor, Katherine Anderson.

Linda Roghaar, because I know there is no better literary agent alive.

Molly Wolf, for her brilliant help, insight, and time.

Frederick W. Shuler, Ph.D., who took an hour of his life to discuss deranged squirrels with me. (Really.)

Knitwear designers everywhere, for being the inspiration for my "Dear Designer." You know I love you anyway.

My patient spouse, Joe Dunphy, and our three daughters, Amanda, Megan, and Samantha Pearl. (Sorry for everything.)

Ken Allen, Lene Andersen, Emma Hogbin, Bonnie McPhee, and anyone else who endured this book's neurotic, mercurial, high-strung birth on the other end of a phone line. (Sorry for that, too.)

Finally, I have to thank the many knitters who have shared their time, stories, and comments. I couldn't do it without you.